THE *little* BOOK FOR *big* WORRIES

DEALING WITH SERIOUS ILLNESS

Israel Bookshop
Publications

THE little BOOK
FOR big WORRIES
DEALING WITH SERIOUS ILLNESS
RABBI Y.Y. RUBINSTEIN

ISBN 978-1-60091-209-2

Book design by Elisheva Appel

Distributed by:
Israel Bookshop Publications
501 Prospect Street / Lakewood, NJ 08701
Tel: (732) 901-3009 / Fax: (732) 901-4012
www.israelbookshoppublications.com
info@israelbookshoppublications.com

Printed in the United States of America

Distributed in Israel by:
Shanky's
Petach Tikva 16
Jerusalem
972-2-538-6936

Distributed in Australia by:
Gold's Book and Gift Company
3- 13 William Street
Balaclava 3183
613-9527-8775

Distributed in Europe by:
Lehmanns
Unit E Viking Industrial Park
Rolling Mill Road,
Jarrow , Tyne & Wear NE32 3DP
44-191-430-0333

Distributed in South Africa by:
Kollel Bookshop
Ivy Common
107 William Road, Norwood
Johannesburg 2192
27-11-728-1822

IN MEMORY OF

DR. ED LEVINE

חנוך ליב בן מרדכי ע״ה

WHO HELPED SO VERY MANY

WITH BIG WORRIES

TO BECOME WELL AGAIN

A dedicated doctor who cared tirelessly

for his patients to whom he always gave hope

A man of great humor, kindness, and humility

who loved and was loved by his family dearly

Dedicated with love by his wife Tanya

and daughters Georgia, Eli, and Anna Levine

IN MEMORY OF

MY GOOD FRIEND,

Irving Hyman

יצחק בן שמשון שאול

WHO HELPED SO MANY.

He was a wonderful and humble man

who was beloved by all.

Dedicated with love by his wife Anne;

children Aaron, Ruth, and Sara;

and all the grandchildren

יחיאל מיכל טווערסקי

כאאמו"ר הרה"צ כמוהר"ר יעקב ישראל זצללה"ה מהארנאסטייפאל

Rabbi Michel Twerski

בס"ד

ר"ח מנחם אב תשע"ב

למע"כ ידידי היקר והחשוב המו"מ כה"ר יהודה יונה רובנשטיין שליט"א

I am delighted once again to offer my approbation to your forthcoming book, The Little Book for BIG Worries . If I could distill my feelings in a few short sentences, they would read as follows: **"The little book for BIG worries" is vintage Rubinstein. Always informative, always inspiring, always engaging, always insightful. Rabbi Rubinstein has two feet on the ground, his mind in heaven, and a giant heart which bridges the two.**

Mazel Tov on another winner. I shall look forward to its publication. Bracha and Hatzlacha.

With deepest respect and affection, I am
Sincerely yours,

Rabbi Michel Twerski

Congregation Beth Jehudah • 3100 N. 52nd Street • Milwaukee, WI 53216 • ph. 414 442-5730 • Fax 414 442-6171
Home Study • 3259 N. 51st Boulevard • Milwaukee, WI 53216 • ph. 414 442-6983 • Fax 414 447-6995

Rabbi Paysach J. Krohn

117-09 85th Avenue • Kew Gardens, NY 11418 (718) 846-6900 • Fax (718) 846-690
e-mail: krohnmohel@brisquest.com • www.brisquest.com

Tamuz 5772/July 2012
Dear Reader;

If you have picked up this book then perhaps you or someone close to you is involved in a serious life crisis. Hopefully it is not you who is in crisis and you are reading this book to help others. However, fear not, for even if it is you, my dear friend Rabbi Yehudah Yonah Rubinstein has come to give you chizuk and a Torah perspective of what is going on in your life.

My favorite sentence in this book is, "The problem is that doctors think they are G-d, and people forget that G-d is a doctor." There are many health issues that Klal Yisroel faces. As Rabbi Rubinstein writes so poignantly, "While one person's Big Worry might be the struggle to bring a child into this world, another fears he will watch one leave it." How does one deal with these situations? There is guidance in this wonderful book.

I find it remarkable that the brocha in Shemoneh Esrei for healing, 'Refaeinu' is the eight brocha. Chazal teach that the brocha was put eighth to be a prayer for boys that are having their bris, which is usually performed on their eight day of life. I would like to suggest an additional reason. The Maharal writes that the number eight symbolizes something that is higher than nature, beyond the conventional. And perhaps therein lies the lesson of the brocha of Refaeinu. Healing is supernatural and can only come about by Hashem who is above nature.

Rabbi Rubinstein takes the patient, the family and concerned friends to that plane above nature. Gently and with a splash of his sense of humor he brings his points home. I am honored to know him and grateful for the opportunity to recommend this wonderful work. May all who read it be inspired and may all who need healing merit complete recovery. And along the way, take this book with you. You will smile as you heal.

Respectfully
Paysach J. Krohn

Acknowledgments

In a book whose title is *The "Little" Book for Big Worries,* it would not be appropriate to make the acknowledgments too lengthy. Nor would it be appropriate not to express my sincere thanks to all of those special individuals who have helped me make the book a reality. I am grateful once again to Rabbi Michel Twerski *shlit"a* of Milwaukee for taking the time to read one of my manuscripts and give me his *haskamah*. My thanks to my dear friend Rabbi Paysach Krohn *shlit"a* for his *haskamah* and interest in this book.

I would also like to express my sincere appreciation to Rabbi Dr. Akiva Tatz and Dr. Fred Glatter for reading the manuscript and employing their medical expertise in matters of medical halachah.

Doctors at the professional level of those who contributed three of the chapters here, are very busy people indeed.

I first met Dr. David Landau when we learned together in the Gateshead yeshivah. His reputation in his field is superb and I would like to express my gratitude for his time and excellent contribution.

Professor Katz and I first met when I came to speak in Houston, Texas. She has made a real and historic contribution to the world of medicine and toward reducing the number of Big Worries that people will have to suffer. Her kindness in becoming part of this little book is very great indeed.

Dr. Andrew Fink and I first met when he was a medical student at Newcastle University and I was in the Gateshead yeshivah. I crossed the river Tyne every week and we studied Torah together. We have remained friends ever since. Once again, I would like to express my thanks to him for giving of his time and for his involvement in the book.

Zahava Farbman of Chai Lifeline helped me enormously with the final — and pretty significant — chapter, suggesting names of individuals and organizations who can direct people with Big Worries toward the addresses where they can find help.

I would like to express my thanks to my dear son, Rabbi Eliyohu Eliezer Rubinstein, who encouraged me to write this book in the first place and contributed many valuable ideas.

Lastly, I would like to thank my dear wife Elisa for her encouragement, enthusiasm, and laughter, and for reading and correcting my writing.

Rabbi Y.Y. Rubinstein
Tammuz 5772

DEDICATED TO:

Sarah bas Esther

Rifka Brocho bas Esther Chaya

Elisheva Perl bas Rochel Adel

Hashem Yisbarach should send all three a *refuah sheleimah.*

Y.Y.R.

The Little Book for Big Worries

DEALING WITH SERIOUS ILLNESS

Introduction

I can't quite remember who, but one *gadol* often gave an unusual kind of blessing to a *chassan* and *kallah* when he spoke at a wedding: "You should have a life full of worries."

I am sure that upon hearing it, many of his listeners would have raised their eyebrows and been more than a little perplexed. Some might even have been offended — after all, it seemed more like a curse than a blessing.

What the *rav* meant was that if you have a life full of worries (as we all do), they will be little worries. He was blessing them that they should have a life in which there is no Big Worry.

We had a normal life full of little worries: raising children, money, family politics, money, community politics, money, school problems, and money.

My wife found a lump. It was technically a breast lump, but it was so high that I thought it more a lower shoulder lump. The doctor who gave us the result of the biopsy was Spanish. I remember her words very clearly, "You have a leetle cancer."

To this day, I am almost amused by her use of the adjective, "leetle." The truth is that there is very little "leetle" about cancer. It is a Big Worry.

A third of human beings contract this disease — there are even forms of it unique to Ashkenazi Jews. While on one of my lecture tours in Chicago, I was asked by two people to write down some thoughts that might be useful in helping people with a Big Worry.

I did so, and called the piece "Big Worries." I published it in my second book, *That's Life,* where the title was changed to, "An Equivalence of Suffering."

Maybe because it was written from the heart more than anything else I have written in the six books I've authored, it seemed to have entered other people's hearts. That is certainly what the Talmud says happens when words come from the heart.

That chapter was requested for inclusion in another book for people struggling with serious illness. It was also published in several Jewish newspapers.

Someone told me of a Manhattan lawyer who sat down at his desk one day in a state of deep depression. His wife had been diagnosed with a very rare form of cancer. Even with all the medical expertise available on the East Coast of the United States, they couldn't find anyone who knew how to treat the disease. Those who had tried, had failed. The lawyer's wife had been sent home to wait for the end.

Sitting on his desk, someone had printed out the article "Big Worries," and although he spent most of his time in a daze, he read it. He got up, put on his coat, and came home to show it to his wife, and they decided to fight some more. They eventually found another doctor who treated her and succeeded where others had failed.

A few weeks ago, I was asked by one of my sons for several copies of "Big Worries" to give to the members of two families whose daughters — who were classmates and best friends — were in opposite rooms from each other in Manchester's Christie Hospital (a cancer treatment hospital). I also gave it to the parents of one of the girls I teach in seminary here in New York. She had been diagnosed with a different, although no less serious, condition.

My son suggested that I expand that chapter into a small handbook that would build on the messages and advice of the original, and would be available to people when they suddenly find they are facing a Big Worry.

I hope and pray that this little book will help a person

whose world abruptly turns itself upside down, when there are many questions and few answers.

It is my hope as well that this book will provide a merit for those three outstanding young ladies and will add to all the prayers and blessings on their behalf. I hope that it will help all the names on a different kind of list (that I wish was not as long as it is), that I include in my prayers three times a day.

I also hope that every new word in this little book will come from the heart and go on to provide guidance to all those who find themselves with a Big Worry, or supporting someone who has discovered that they have one.

Lastly, I would like to express my gratitude to *Hashem Yisbarach,* our true Doctor Who continually held me up when I thought I would fall, and gave me the privilege to inspire others in need to recognize, *Ani Hashem rofecha* — "I am Hashem Who heals you."

CHAPTER 1

When a Big Worry Begins

I will be perfectly honest with you. I am a coward. I am also quite a hypochondriac. So when I found a lump on my arm, I was sure that it was malignant, and at the same time terrified to show it to the doctor. I eventually did so. It was called a lipoma, which is a cluster of little globules of fat under the skin. It is about the size of a fingertip. I had it removed, and when I grew others (fourteen in all) years later, I had them removed too.

The medical term for a lump is a tumor. It comes from the Latin word that means swelling. Most tumors are just like mine, completely harmless. Of course that doesn't mean you won't worry about it if you find one. I did. But diseases are more successfully treated the sooner they are found. Pretending something isn't there when you know it is will not make it go away, so the sooner you can be told that it is nothing to worry about — or that it is something that needs to be treated — the better.

Apart from that very practical reason, there is another. As the Talmud teaches, much worse than receiving bad news is *worrying* about receiving bad news.

One of my best friends looked across the table at me in shul one Friday night with tears in his eyes. I took him aside and asked him what was wrong. He told me that he had just been diagnosed with cancer of the kidney. We both stood crying with no words to say.

After Shabbos he went to see a specialist who looked at his X-rays and other test results. "Who told you this was cancer?" he inquired. It was not. Doctors make mistakes. Doctors are human.

When a Big Worry threatens, it does not mean that it *is* a Big Worry. It might be nothing. For whatever reasons Hashem had, He decided you needed to have a scare. We will talk about why later in this book in the chapter called, "Why *Do* Very Bad Things Happen to Very Good People?"

Rabbi Eliyahu Dessler points out in his essay, "Miracles and Nature," that Hashem is more likely to make a miracle occur when it does not have to fly in the face of what science and medicine say.

We usually believe and trust in the world and its experts' opinions and predictions. If we are being honest with ourselves, it is often hard for us to overcome what medical science says and believe that Hashem will overturn it, unless we are on a very high spiritual level.

Our faith and confidence in science is strengthened when bolstered by medical predictions and pronouncements. Therefore, our chances of having miracles performed for us are greater prior to our receiving science's verdict, when the outcome will not be perceived as contrary to nature.

The nerve-wracking period of tests and waiting for results often tests us in a totally different way. This twilight time is when our prayers can most easily produce a huge miracle. It is the time when we pray with more sincerity than we have ever achieved in our entire lives. In fact, that might well be the reason Hashem decided we needed to experience a scare in the first place.

The escape of the word "Phew!" we might utter when a doctor tells us everything was okay after all, might allow us to believe that there was indeed nothing to worry about. At that moment we might be so keen to flee the hospital and forget about what we just went through, that we won't consider that maybe there really *was* a lot to worry about. Our prayers and the prayers of those who care about us allowed Hashem to change what the doctors saw under the microscope.

> **Waiting for results is terrible, very terrible...but it is also the best time to ask Hashem to make the wait produce good news.**

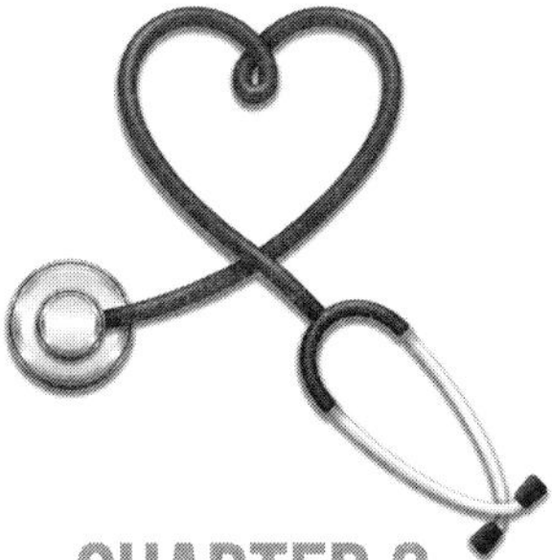

CHAPTER 2

Big Worry Confirmed

If a Big Worry turns out to be well founded, you will find yourself part of a process and sucked into a system with many protocols.

I recall a meeting to which I was invited to attend to explain what my experiences had been when we found ourselves in "the system." Local doctors wanted to hear things that had gone right, and just as importantly, things that hadn't. In the vast majority of cases, healthcare professionals try very hard to do the best they can.

When these processes, systems, and protocols all

spring to life, although they will usually be explained to you, you will still struggle to absorb and understand them. The more you do understand, the better you can determine which course of action works for you.

Protocols and systems are constructed, like most rules, because they work and apply to most people. If you are not "most people," they may fail spectacularly both medically and personally.

The newest innovation in treatment addresses an amazing and little-known fact. No two cancers are the same. Even two people suffering from precisely the same disease at the same stage are essentially suffering from two different diseases. How it behaves in your body is specific to you. It really is "your cancer."

New treatments take the specific "genetic fingerprint" of every person's unique cancer and how it is behaving in their body, and design a patient-specific treatment. It is obvious that this promises a huge advance in treatment success rates.

The same holds true for the personality of the patient. What society in general — and medical society in particular — believes may be the best approach, might not fit you.

My children all attended the same religious Jewish elementary school in Manchester. The government sent inspectors to monitor the performance of the students. The children were given a standardized IQ test, and the results showed that they had all scored very poorly.

This did not square with the performance they expected to find. The IQ test was reviewed, and was discovered to be the source of the problem. It did not fit the children. Many questions were "culture-bound."

The answer they were looking for to the question, "Fish and...?" was "Chips"! Religious Jewish children wrote, "Fish and Mayonnaise"!

Different cultures and religions have different customs, practices, and norms.

As we said, in the majority of cases, healthcare professionals try very hard to do the best they can. That "best" will be the best as they see it and may sometimes be the worst as we do.

Doctors and nurses may honestly believe that they should not resuscitate someone who is very ill even if they could do so. Why bring them back to more pain? They may sincerely believe that speeding someone's departure from that pain either by omission or commission is a noble and good thing to do.

We don't.

(I should add that as long as the goal is pain relief and not euthanasia, most halachic authorities agree that treatment that relieves pain, even if there is an increased risk to life, is allowed.)

In the midst of confusing and fearsome news whose ramifications you do not comprehend, you are likely not to know how to make sure the system works for and with your needs. You need to speak to people who do. You will need to speak to them many times as your story unfolds. At the end of this book, you will find a list of organizations and individuals who help people navigate their way around and through systems and protocols to make sure your treatment fits you.

> **In the midst of confusing and fearsome news, you need to speak to people who understand you and are familiar with the procedures and protocols you are being introduced to. Make sure you are helped by those who know how to make the system work for and with your needs.**

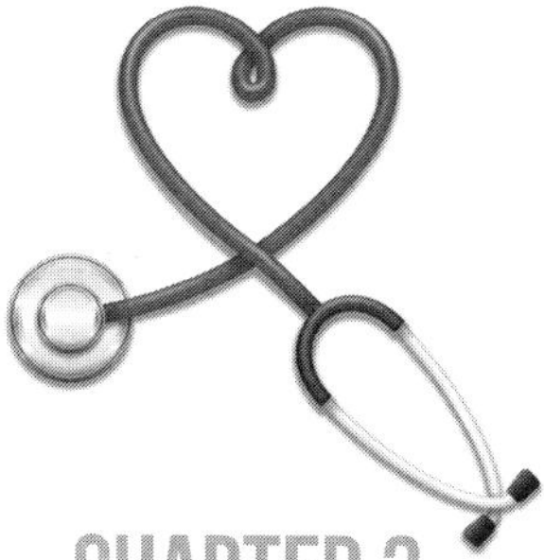

CHAPTER 3

Finding the Right Someone to Talk To

Once the protocols we discussed in the last chapter start to work with you, there is a different and essential aspect of advice you need to secure.

There are two words in English, derived from the same Greek word *pathos,* which means "to feel," that sound almost the same: sympathy and empathy.

Sympathy means to feel sorry for someone. Empathy means to feel as though you *are* the person suffering. It is what the *mussar* works say is essential in order to perform the mitzvah of *nosei b'ol im chaveiro* — "carrying your friend's burden together with him." You have to be as one with him, able to feel and carry his pain.

The Gemara famously says that if you visit a sick person, you take away one-sixtieth of his illness. But only if a certain condition is met.

There are two explanations of what that condition is, one by Rashi and the other by the Ran. The visitor either has to be the same age as the person he is visiting, or have the same *mazel* — in other words, the same life experience. That way, the person visiting easily sees himself as though it was him lying ill in bed. After all, with the same background, age or circumstance, there is no discernible reason why it could not be him lying there. As there is only an exact amount of pain ordained for a person from Heaven, in feeling part of that pain, *you* took it instead of him, and that fraction of pain is no longer available for him.

When you have a Big Worry, you need to be able to have access to people who will not just sympathize, but empathize as well.

I knew a woman who was a counselor in a hospital burn unit. Many times, this smartly dressed and attractive woman of forty-something would sit beside someone who was very badly burned indeed. Some had no facial features left. As she began to talk, she often experienced a very angry reaction, "What do you know about what I'm going through; have you ever been burned?!"

It is difficult to express in writing just the amount of anger and fury with which their words and sentiments were sometimes expressed. The counselor remained calm and quietly replied, "No, I have never been burned, but both my parents were burned in Auschwitz."

When she said that, the barrier was breached, and the patients would allow her to help them.

I call it an "equivalence of suffering." When you have a Big Worry, you need to get help from someone who has an equivalence of suffering.

Thank G-d, most people, especially under the age of about thirty-five, are not likely to have an equivalence of suffering under their belts. Yet often, especially if they are a *rav* or a *rebbetzin,* they will have to deal with people with Big Worries who are in very great emotional pain indeed. These few pages are in part an attempt to offer some insight that might help, at the very least, good people from making bad mistakes while attempting to do their best.

> **When you have a Big Worry, you need to be able to speak to someone who has an equivalence of suffering.**

CHAPTER 4

A Simple but Invaluable Piece of Advice

My wife and I were blessed by *Hashem Yisbarach* in so many ways. One of them was both of us having a sense of humor. Medical research proves, by the way, that people with cancer who can laugh about their situation have an enormously better chance of defeating the disease than those who can't.

Early on in our story, when the word "leetle" was

looming very large indeed, one of our very good friends, Rebbetzin Liba Gottlieb, phoned from Jerusalem. She gave us a great piece of advice — "Keep an Idiot Book!"

She continued, "Lots of people will say lots of really stupid things. Write them down and see which is the current dumbest comment."

We didn't exactly do that, but we did keep a "Top Ten." Every now and again, a particularly talented person — who is to tact what Joseph Stalin was to democracy — would come along and depose the current number one.

A certain woman told my wife, "You know, Mrs. Cohen has the same illness as you, and she got a *brachah* that she should live to see all her children married. Why are you marrying off your children so quickly?"

This was said with absolute sincerity and curiosity.

Da Da! Yes, ladies and gentlemen... The new Number One... Mrs. ***** from ******!

She was "topped" a few times since then, but she is still firmly there in pride of place in the top five. Such folk really don't mean to cause distress and usually haven't a clue as to how inappropriate their "advice" is.

Now, instead of hurting or upsetting you, these outrageous suggestions might just cause a barely discernible smile to appear on your face as you make a mental note to adjust and amend the list in your book.

Keep an Idiot Book!

CHAPTER 5

A Few Simple Rules

When you are talking to someone who has a Big Worry, you are walking in a minefield. It might be that on that particular day, she or he might be in a state of mind where they are very sensitive and almost nothing will be the right thing to say.

Don't "beat yourself up" because you failed and said the wrong thing. It may well be impossible, sometimes, to say the right thing.

Before you call or visit, speak to the one closest to the person with the Big Worry and find out what his state of mind is at the time. He might be in the mood to hear encouraging words or simply welcome the chance to tell someone what is happening. He might not want to receive visitors at all. Asking the "experts" — the spouse or adult children — is the first and safest step.

There are a few other rules, which almost always hold true.

Mention people you know or know of, who had the same condition twenty or thirty years ago and are fine today. Hope is the most important weapon of all. My wife had a second cousin who had cancer seven times over thirty years — in both breasts, bone, and skin, to name a few. She died at age seventy of a heart attack.

Her name was Dora and we think of her often. There are people, lots of people, who beat and vanquish this disease and other diseases too.

Someone I know faced setback after setback following her initial diagnosis. Then the doctors told her that there would have to be further and more radical surgery. When I and everyone else heard this latest, dark chapter, I was plunged into despair and wondered how the young person going through this could deal with this recent and most cruel blow.

At that time, she received a phone call from someone who had been the same age when he was given the same terrible diagnosis. He, too, was told that he would have to undergo the same radical surgery. During that phone call, he described exactly the emotions he had felt then and which the new sufferer was feeling and coping with now.

What helped to heal the wound that was yet to be inflicted was the fact that this guy with the identical diagnosis was now in good health, and he assured her that she, too, would be able to function perfectly well afterward. He was able to encourage her by sharing that he went on to have a normal and happy life, and that today he is a grandfather.

> **Listen out for "Doras" and file them away so you can introduce them to people who might need to meet them on their quest to become "Doras" too.**

CHAPTER 6

It's All about the Words

In the previous chapter, I used the words "vanquish" and "beat." Words are important. Words scare. Remission is a word that does not sound confident or not confident enough. I don't use it.

Once, during my wife's illness, she was in the local hospital because of a fluid build-up in her lungs. One day I received a call from a nurse to come in, as the lung specialist had given her bad news.

I was terrified that the recent scans had revealed that the disease had moved to the lungs. In fact, this doctor had different bad news. He told my wife that she had less than two weeks to live.

This was all done without any prior consultation with the patient's representative (myself), and when I arrived, the doctor shared his prognosis with me. I didn't think — I didn't think the way a Jew should. I was in shock. I don't have to tell you that the hour or so we spent together afterward was the most painful and difficult of our lives.

When the oncologist who was treating her in the Christie heard what this lung specialist said, he sent us a message that he strongly disagreed, and wanted us back in his hospital. He had certainly not given up hope.

This message was delivered to our bedside by a junior doctor. She added the caveat that her boss, the lung specialist, thought that it was "crazy," and that there was no hope in reversing the situation.

Once you have "thrown in the towel," it is very difficult — almost impossible — to pick it up again. Once reconciled to dying, a person becomes ready and almost willing to die. Now, we were being invited to start fighting all over again.

My wife asked me what I thought we should do, and I told her that the decision had to be hers. There obviously had to be the will to fight; otherwise the best efforts of our oncologist would be futile.

After a while my wife replied, "I suppose I am *mechuyav* (obliged) to carry on." This was, of course, the right reply, the one the Torah would expect. She was not, though, able to give it with the determination that would make the "carrying on" successful. The damage of the lung specialist's words had overwhelmed her as it had me.

Before we left the hospital, I phoned our own general practitioner and related all that had happened. I asked him to get hold of the lung specialist and tell him to get back to my wife's room and "un-say" what he had said the day before. The lung specialist did try, and at our oncologist's insistence, started her on steroids. (He had not given her this medication until now as he was quite convinced that she was going to die.)

The next day, she was transferred to Manchester's famous Christie Hospital, home to the discovery of tamoxifen, the breast cancer drug.

A junior doctor who initially saw my wife confided that she didn't think that her boss (our optimistic oncologist) had realized how bad Yaffa's condition was, and she also thought that there was almost no hope at all.

At the Christie, I had a friend who had been a superb support for both of us. He was a senior oncologist, and I had alerted him to our story and arranged for him to visit my wife and challenge the pessimistic prognosis she had been given. All this helped a little bit to repair the damage, but only a little.

The next day, one of my sons had a much better idea — to ask Rav Mattisyahu Salamon *shlit"a* for his help. I am a *talmid* of Rav Mattisyahu; he spoke at our wedding.

At a prearranged time, while my wife's sister and I were at her bedside, my cell phone rang. I handed it to my wife and she looked perplexed as to who it might be. As she put the phone to her ear and heard Rav Mattisyahu's voice, I watched a miracle take place.

He did not begin by speaking gently and kindly to her; he was quite stern. He told her to remember who she was and what she was. He insisted that she recall that it is *Hashem Yisbarach* Who decides when a person passes away, not doctors. *Then* he spoke gently and kindly to her.

I don't know if you have ever watered a plant that has been wilting through lack of moisture. In a few minutes, it comes to life before your eyes. Yaffa came to life, and the dreadful damage of the specialist's frightful words was at last undone.

Rav Mattisyahu phoned my wife every day after that. Yaffa also received calls from Lady Jacobovitz *a"h* and *tbl"c*, Rebbetzin Ehrentreu (Dayan Ehrentreu's wife) from London, and her fight back to life was well on its way.

At that time, I got a call from a student of mine in New Jersey, who comes with her husband to hear me speak whenever I am visiting in their state. She is a wise woman and I already cited an example of her wisdom in my book, *Dancing Through Time*. She called after receiving an e-mail I had sent out requesting our friends' *tefillos*, and when I told her the story which appears in the last few paragraphs, she said, "You know, Rabbi Rubinstein, the problem is that doctors sometimes think they're gods... and people forget that G-d is a Doctor!"

Two months later, my wife and I spent a few days away in England's beautiful Lake District. When we parked at Marks and Spencer's (where else?), I offered to fetch a wheelchair for Yaffa, who was still very weak. She refused and instead took one of the shopping trolleys and marched around the store filling it. I watched her in complete admiration. We had both, for a while, forgotten to "remember who she was."

Writing this now, I think this is a tale worth retelling. And those wise words should be engraved in every Jewish mind: "The problem is that sometimes doctors think they're gods...and people forget that G-d is a Doctor."

There is another obvious lesson to draw from this story. People who mean a lot to the patient and can play a significant role in their lives should be involved in helping them get well.

(By the way, the doctor at the Christie who refused to give up is one of the greatest people I have ever met. He is brilliant in his field and has excellent people skills. I am more grateful to him than my writing abilities could express.)

The problem is that sometimes doctors think they're gods...and people forget that G-d is a Doctor.

CHAPTER 7

Two Things to Watch Out For

Be very wary, though, of those who are themselves survivors of a Big Worry and want to come and encourage someone else.

Such people fall into two categories: those who come because they want to help the sufferer, and those who come because they need to help *themselves*. In assuring others that they will overcome obstacles as they have themselves, they are actually reassuring themselves, not the person who is ill. This second category of "well-wishers" need to *hear themselves* saying those words.

The person receiving the visit will know the difference. The first will help; the second will not and could cause much damage.

I mentioned before that sometimes finding the right words will prove impossible. We can't know what is going on in the sufferer's mind at any given time. Try to avoid clichés. The sentiments behind the cliché might well be sincere and genuine, but the formulistic nature of the words will rob them of the appearance of sincerity.

Be wary of being too encouraging. Phrases like, "You'll be fine," can be damaging.

The person might well be thinking, "What on earth does he/she know — has she ever felt pain like this?"

> **Survivors of a Big Worry who want to come and encourage someone else fall into two categories: those who want to come to help the sufferer and those who need to come because they need to help *themselves*.**

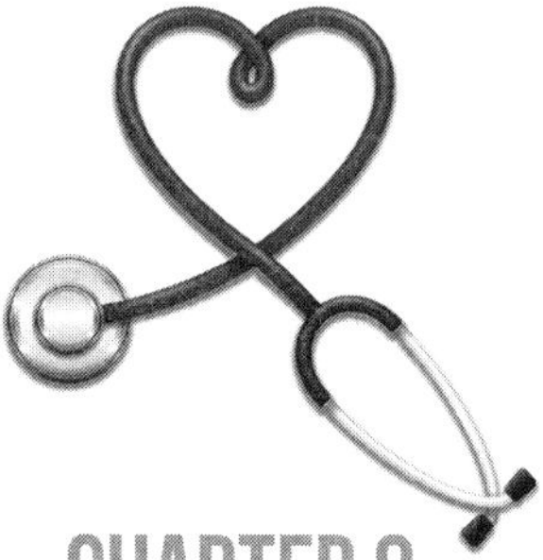

CHAPTER 8

There Are Different Rules for People with Big Worries

Whenever there is confirmation of a Big Worry, the reaction of almost any person is, "Why me? What have I done wrong to deserve this?"

Those are two questions that are mandated by the Talmud at the beginning of *Maseches Brachos*. You are supposed to ask them when bad things happen. But sometimes, asking them can be as destructive as the diagnosis itself!

A friend of mine once asked the *rav* of Gateshead, Rabbi Betzalel Rakow *zt"l,* a question in halachah. My friend was involved in *kiruv rechokim* (outreach) at the time, and he was surprised by the leniency of the answer he received. The *rav* noted his surprise and said, "There is a different *Shulchan Aruch* (set of laws) for *kiruv rechokim*!"

If I might paraphrase the *rav's* words, "There is a different *Shulchan Aruch* for Big Worries!"

One night, when my wife's first course of chemotherapy was about to begin, I awoke to find her sobbing uncontrollably. Her state left me emotionally crippled, helpless and unable to think of anything to say. She asked, "Why me? What have I done wrong to deserve this?"

It was five o'clock in the morning and I suggested we go downstairs and phone Rav Mattisyahu Salamon in Lakewood. This was what he told my wife:

"I always say that this disease is a *hemshech* (continuation) of the *g'zar din* (Heavenly decree) against Klal Yisrael from the Second World War. You would not say that someone who found himself in Bergen-Belsen or Dachau had done anything personally to deserve being there; rather it was a decree against the Jewish people as a whole. It's exactly the same with this disease. Victims are not suffering for what *they* have done wrong. It is a *g'zar din* against all of Klal Yisrael...the whole Jewish people."

Rav Mattisyahu has, by the way, an equivalence of suffering — his mother and brother had this disease.

The exact same proportion of the Jewish people become ill with cancer as were killed in the Holocaust: a third. People are often reduced to looking exactly like concentration camp inmates, emaciated with shaved heads. The emotional and psychological toll is similar too. We even refer to them sometimes by the same term — survivors.

In this specific case, the Gemara's formula for individuals to ask, "Why me?" is not appropriate. "Why US?" is instead the real question.

People who are ill with a Big Worry need to be encouraged not to "beat themselves up."

Reb Shlomo Brevda *shlit"a* went to visit a friend of ours who suffers from multiple sclerosis. She is a *rebbetzin* who cried to him bitterly that she could not *daven* properly. Whenever she tried, her mind just went blank. He told her, "My dear lady, you are just busy keeping your head above the water; no wonder you can't *daven*!"

The classic Jewish responses might not be appropriate or at least not appropriate just then.

There is a different *Shulchan Aruch* for Big Worries!

The laws of Shabbos and other *halachos* fall away to help a seriously ill person. The same is true with *hashkafos* (Jewish views and perspectives). The right words at the right time, the right thoughts at the right time, can heal.

The wrong thoughts or words can do profound harm. The right thoughts or words *at the wrong time,* can cause harm too.

The greatest weapon is hope. The greatest "delivery system" for that weapon is *seichel* (common sense) and wisdom.

There is a different *Shulchan Aruch* for Big Worries!

CHAPTER 9

More about Words

There has been enough in the recent media — both Jewish and secular — about evolving medical attitudes toward seriously ill people.

There was an excellent piece a while back in the *Jewish Observer* about "Do Not Resuscitate" instructions given by doctors without any consultation with the patient's family.

I was once in Har Nof in Jerusalem visiting my good friend Rabbi Professor Dovid Gottlieb *shlit"a*. Someone came over and asked me if I was Rabbi Y.Y. Rubinstein. I was able, with more or less near certainty, to reply that I was.

He looked rather embarrassed and said, "You won't remember me...but you used to teach me at Jewish Youth Study Groups." (JYSG was a UK outreach organization roughly equivalent to NCSY in the States.)

He continued, "I just want you to know that I am everything I am today because of you!"

He shook my hand, and after he walked away, Rabbi Gottlieb turned and asked me, "Do you know who that is?" I could honestly reply that I hadn't a clue. Rabbi Gottlieb looked at me, slowly nodded his head and announced, "Psssss!"

In case you are unfamiliar with *Chareidi*-speak, "Psssss!" means "Wow!" only more so. "Psssss!" is a sort of triple or quadruple "Wow!" It suggests something or someone very exceptional indeed.

Rabbi Gottlieb told me that this young rabbi was exactly that — very exceptional.

Now at this point you might feel that writing this down demonstrates on my part a certain lack of humility and modesty. Nothing could be further from the truth.

This story gives no credit to me at all. I had not and have not a clue who this "Psssss!" was or is. I can tell you of many young people who became close to my wife and me through this organization and then went on to achieve great things. Many actually did become rabbis and *rebbetzins*.

The point is that this rabbi (who I am told is a leading

expert in medical halachah and uses that expertise to help many sick people) heard something I said.

He listened. I was merely repeating the great ideas and concepts of *gedolim* whose words I have studied. His listening meant that he chose to internalize those messages, and was able to grow and become a "Psssss!"

A *shiur*, a sentence, an idea, or even a word can change a life.

We have to be alert to messages medical professionals want to impart. They might have determined that there is no point in prolonging a life whose quality has been significantly diminished. They might act to deny us the opportunity of hearing a few words or even many words that could change our lives, words that need to be said and need to be heard. They may rob us of a day, a week, a month, or even years.

At the beginning of our journey, when we were lucky enough to find our superb oncologist, I spoke to him privately. I explained that we were Orthodox Jews. I told him that we needed hope more than anything. If there was any bad news, I asked if he could tell me first so I could judge when, how, and if to pass it on. I don't know what the normal protocols would have said about my request, but he was happy to comply. He had already become our friend, and his support and agreement on this issue was an enormously positive weapon in fighting the disease.

We have to be alert to messages medical professionals want to impart. A sentence, an idea, or even a single word can change a life for the better or the worse.

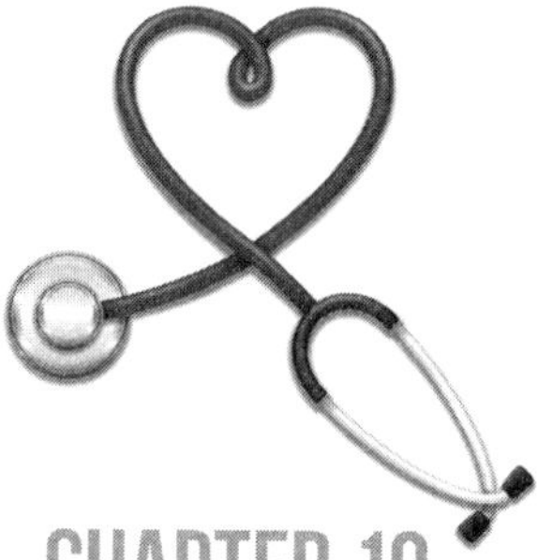

CHAPTER 10

Be Aware that Sometimes Doctors May Not be Helping You

Although most of the medical staff I dealt with were outstanding and sympathetic to how we needed things done, not all of them are.

Strategies for dealing with medical fashion or ideas that are contrary to our beliefs are an essential ingredient in beating illness and disease.

I once received a call from one of my *talmidim* who was studying at a university. He comes from a non-religious family, and has achieved remarkable growth; he is truly quite exceptional.

When he phoned me from London, he was in a very distressed state. A close relative had been in the hospital for routine tests, and had unexpectedly died.

He needed to ascertain what were the right things to do *al pi halachah* (according to Jewish law). I told him to contact the family rabbi to make sure the body was not left unattended in the hospital. I also told him to try his best to avoid a post-mortem autopsy.

Ten minutes later, he called to say that the rabbi had not been able to help.

A very close friend of mine in Manchester is heavily involved in the *chevra kaddisha* activities, both locally and nationally. I gave my *talmid* his number and assured him that he would help.

Together with others, this particular activist had managed to convince the authorities in the Manchester area to accept a magnetic resonance scan (MRI) instead of an autopsy. From a halachic point of view, this is a superb advance. Any unnecessary procedures on a dead body offends Jewish law and Jewish sensibilities.

The next day, the young man phoned again to explain that my friend had indeed helped and an MRI scan had been arranged. The problem, however, was the next of kin — his father. He was opposed to — what seemed to him — a most abnormal business.

My friend had suggested that I phone and speak to his

dad, who had a reputation as a tough character.

I phoned, and started by conveying my sympathy before explaining the reason for my call. He was not at all happy at my suggestion of a scan. He was not used to talking with rabbis. He was not used to seeing things from a halachic perspective. My suggestion was alien to him and he objected to someone he had never met invading his grief.

At one point, in what was a difficult conversation for both of us, I commented, "I suppose that ultimately, the question of avoiding an autopsy is a religious one."

Immediately I received a blast down the phone, "What do you mean *ultimately*? It is *totally* a religious question!"

But he was wrong; it wasn't and it isn't.

A few months before, the head of one of Manchester's best-known *yeshivos* sent me a message. He wanted me to speak on behalf of his school to the BBC!

When I heard those three letters I was baffled. What did a *Chareidi mosad* (institution) have to do with the BBC? I was soon to find out.

Just before the *zman* (semester) was due to start, the yeshivah's building had been used for a camp. There had been "high jinks" on the last night of the camp and some of the young folk had raided the kitchen for a midnight feast. The cook, who usually keeps the kitchen clean and tidy, came in to find quite a mess.

Her day was just about to get a whole lot worse.

An hour later the food inspector from the local authority turned up to conduct an unannounced visit. She had brought with her a BBC film crew to record the visit. The *rabbanim* allowed them all to come in and, given the antics of the previous night's campers, there was lots for the inspector to be unhappy about, and lots to record on film.

Now the head of the *mosad* wanted my help. A month had passed and the food inspector was soon to return, and she wanted once more to bring the BBC.

I met with the *rabbanim* and we discussed whether or not to let the cameras back. I wondered why they had let them in, in the first place. They *had* to admit the inspector; they did not have to admit the BBC. When I asked the *rabbanim* why they had let the media in, they were honestly as baffled as I was. "I just don't know why we did," one of the *rabbanim* exclaimed while shaking his head.

It was agreed that the second visit was an opportunity to correct the misrepresentation of the first, and so the whole *mosad*, including its *talmidim*, set about rendering it spotless. My job was to talk to the cameras and explain why the first visit had found such a mess.

The food inspector and the BBC returned. While I was sitting and chatting to the film crew, they told me their previous assignment was to film inside a morgue, and an autopsy. None of them were Jewish or at all religious, and still the cameraman said, "I sincerely hope to heaven that no one does anything like that to me when I die. The way they treat a dead body is a total disgrace!"

He went on to elaborate horrific details of callous disregard to the dignity of the dead person who was treated more like a slab of meat in a butcher's shop than a human being. This account received nods of agreement from his colleagues.

The second visit of the cameras more than undid the damage of the first, and it also planted a memory I was able to call up in my conversation with my *talmid's* father.

"It isn't *totally* a religious question," I replied to the blast down the phone. I then went on to share the cameraman's story with him, even telling him when he could see the grizzly broadcast on television.

I finished speaking and he was still very unhappy. My very best efforts were clearly in vain, so I apologized once again for having phoned at such a painful time and then hung up.

When I explained to my friend from the *chevra kaddisha* that I had failed to persuade the next of kin to allow the MRI to take place, he was bitterly disappointed.

Although the Manchester authorities were happy to recognize MRI scans instead of autopsies, my friend had not succeeded with the London authorities — until this case, that is. To his amazement, this time the London coroner had yielded to his request. Now he would have to go back and tell him that the Jewish family had refused and all his previous efforts to have scanning established nationwide would be undone.

Five minutes later the phone rang again and it was my *talmid.* There had been a change of heart and his father had now given his consent!

I phoned my friend back to tell him the news, and as I did so, I realized I now had the answer that the *rabbanim* of the *mosad* could not provide. I now knew why they had inexplicably allowed a BBC film crew into their building; so that I would have the opportunity to hear from one of them words that would change a "tough character's" mind!

The outcome of this episode was that with the precedent set by this case, London also went on to accept MRI scans instead of autopsies.

Doctors, nurses, and other healthcare professionals usually see things through the lens of the system and discipline within which they work and were trained. The view they have received is the one they are likely to pass on to you. This story showed me that what people believe to be the case and the reality of certain procedures might be very different from what the reality actually is. Medical protocols speak at length about treating human beings with respect before and after death. Having been the rabbi to a quarter of a century's worth of medical students, I know that there is often a large gap between what is supposed to happen and what does.

It may be the fashion not to resuscitate or offer ongoing treatment that they believe pointless, or to insist on an autopsy. You may receive sincere and passionate pleas for you to come around and view things their way. You may find yourself under great pressure at a time when your emotional resources are almost drained.

Often, though, there are ways to persuade doctors, nurses, and other healthcare professionals to see things differently — to see things our way — but you will need to access and recruit those in our communities who know how to go about getting them to do so.

> **You have to be in touch at the outset of a Big Worry with those who have dealt with them before and know what a Jewish response requires. You need someone who can cajole, persuade, and if necessary, fight for you.**

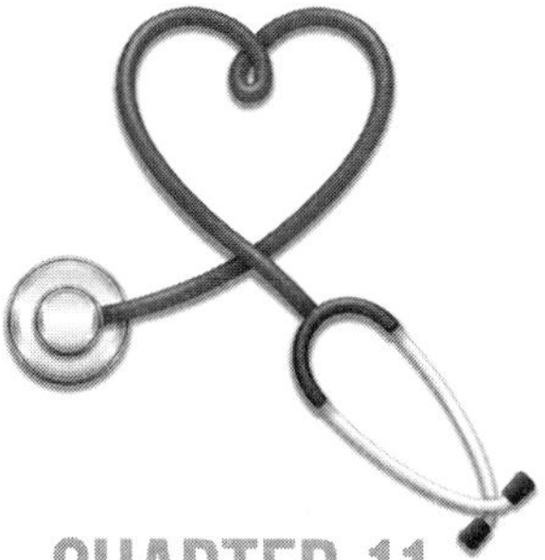

CHAPTER 11

How to Make a Patient Feel Comfortable

There is an area in dealing with Big Worries that demands a unique approach from each individual.

I once read about someone who was suffering from an incurable disease. His doctor had offered him an operation that would extend his life by six months, but would be very painful. He went to discuss his options with Reb Moshe Feinstein *zt"l*. The patient was a religious Jew and Reb Moshe told him, "You know already what you're supposed to do... but I can't tell you that you *should* do it."

That story is a very important lesson when dealing with people with a Big Worry. They have to be allowed to deal with their situation in the way that is best for them. They might well ask for advice: medical, spiritual, spousal, or whatever, but ultimately they have to make their own decisions. The people offering the sought advice have to understand their personalities and abide by their individual preferences.

At the beginning of our story, my wife was very open with her condition. Some friends organized an evening where women were invited to a school hall to pray for her recovery. Hundreds came. The numbers were so huge that people had to participate by standing outside in the playground. Yaffa drew tremendous support and encouragement from this.

The types of women who came were also a source of encouragement. *Every* type of woman came. Some were Chassidic with a little hat on top of their *sheitel*, and some were *Litvish* and had *sheitels* without hats. Some were *Mizrachi* and wore scarves either all the time or just for this occasion, and some never covered their hair at all.

I know of at least one young woman who had been a student of ours while at university and had told me many times that she didn't believe in G-d. She was there reciting Tehillim with the rest, crying her eyes out.

Other people I know who have a Big Worry prefer that no one knows about it.

Of course that means that prayers will not be said for them by hundreds — in our case thousands — of others. We know that prayers can change everything and leave doctors scratching their heads.

That, however, is how *they* are able to deal with their situation and that is how all of us who are near those individuals have to proceed.

Once all the facts have been laid before the patient, as long as the options are halachically valid, you have to allow them to choose which path and approach works best for them.

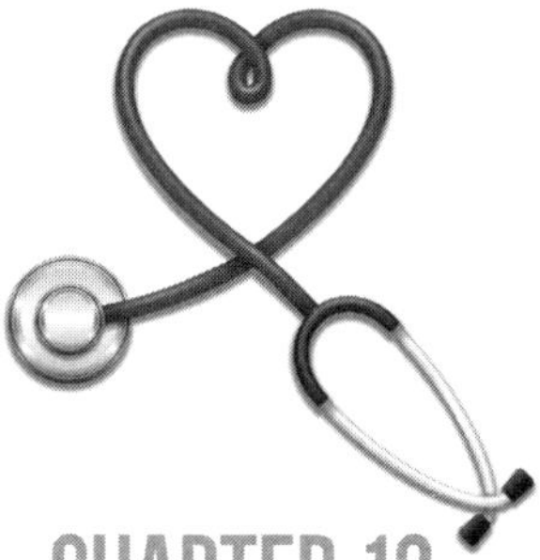

CHAPTER 12

Desperate People are Desperate to Believe Things that Offer Hope

An important caveat applies to the previous chapter.

There is no one as vulnerable as someone who is going through the emotional turmoil of finding themselves seriously ill. Their family will be almost as vulnerable as them.

A number of years ago, I was invited by the BBC to

appear on a TV show to challenge someone who was selling Kabbalah to the masses, Jewish and non-Jewish. The BBC had arranged a secret filming of this person and his organization's activities. Specially "blessed" water, which possessed "mystical powers," was guaranteed to cure a rich man (who had been sent along with a hidden camera) of his prostate cancer.

This same person had sold a set of *Zohar* to a non-Jewish woman who was dying of cancer, assuring her that all she needed to do was run her finger over the words and she would be cured.

Desperate people do desperate things. This lady bought the prized set of *Zohar* for a mere $10,000. This edition usually costs $100. He sold her a *mezuzah*, too, for an obscene amount that would be laughable if it weren't so very sad. She started to run her finger over the print for two weeks until she no longer could, and died.

There are, though, legitimate alternative therapies, which can and should be used in conjunction with mainstream therapies. Almost all doctors will be comfortable with these as long as they do not interfere with the essential treatments that are being given.

If they do, then we should view the suggestion to use them with the utmost skepticism. When the Torah tells us to "guard your lives very much," the Vilna Gaon says that the word *me'od* (very much) means to the "nth degree."

The Talmud teaches that if you have a "maybe" and a

"definite," you always opt for the definite.

Alternative treatments that may help and do not interfere or disrupt the "definite" are a useful addition as long as they come with the blessing and endorsement of the doctors and experts dealing with the Big Worry. They should never become replacements for treatments that medical science honestly believes may help.

Let me repeat this point. If the alternative therapy, massage, acupuncture, etc., complements and can run concurrently with orthodox medicine, then you should consider and probably welcome them. If it does not, stay away from something which interferes with our application of the Torah telling us to "guard your lives very much...to the nth degree."

Someone asked me recently if they should use an alternative therapy in a case of their young son's illness.

Remember, no one is as vulnerable as someone who is going through the emotional turmoil of finding themselves seriously ill. Their family will be almost as vulnerable as them. Desperate people do desperate things. Desperate people want to believe things that offer hope.

I asked for details of the alternative treatment. It turned out that the alternative treatment practitioner insisted that the family refuse part of the chemotherapy regime being offered by the hospital, and that his miracle cure be given instead.

I suggested that firstly, the family discuss it with their doctor. They did so. He was very kind and understanding. Oncologists know that desperate people want to believe things that offer hope. He told them of a case he was involved with once, similar to this one. The doctor asked if he could get hold of some of the wonder drug that was being offered.

The family procured some for him and he had it analyzed. It contained, as promised, only natural ingredients. The natural ingredients had high levels of naturally occurring steroids. These agents are used routinely in cancer treatment and indeed attack cancer cells and make the patient look and feel better — for a while.

They do not deal with the source of the disease. They do not attack that. Worse still, when the temporary respite is over, the cancer is strengthened as a result of having been exposed to those very steroids.

The doctor told the family, "I can give you those very steroids now if you like and you will see immediate improvement. The test results will also show the disease in retreat. I will have done absolutely nothing, though, to cure your son's cancer. It will come back."

Even though desperate people want to believe things that offer hope, this family understood that instead of offering a cure for their son, this "alternative" offered the opposite.

I might add that it also saved them the $40,000 that the possessor of this "breakthrough" and "cure" asked for his treatment.

It actually could be that the person selling this product might even genuinely believe that it works and is the "real deal."

It hardly needs to be said that there exist many unscrupulous people who know that what they are offering to do is nothing more than cruel and cynical exploitation.

The Torah explains the laws of someone who has the disease called *tzara'as*. He will have certain symptoms and signs that show that this condition, caused by a spiritual malaise, is affecting him.

Reb Yerucham Levovitz *zt"l* says in his commentary that the Torah is teaching that *tumah* (ritual impurity) has signs and symptoms.

He cites the analogy of a barn filled with grain. Looking from the outside, you will see that some of the grain will have pushed its way through the cracks between the boards of the barn's wall. You may have to look carefully and closely, but what's inside will come out.

A Jewish person I was recently alerted to offers a cure for cancer on a very impressive and professionally produced website. He has letters after his name that proclaim legitimate medical credentials. They may indeed be legitimate. There was even a clever insinuation that some great rabbis endorsed and recommended him.

Desperate people desperate to believe things that offer hope will feel reassured by all of this.

You may have to look carefully and closely, but what's on the inside will come out.

I looked into this case carefully, and the fact that this person was a charlatan was not too hard to establish. A couple of phone calls showed there were no rabbinic endorsements.

If you are going through a Big Worry, you probably won't be able to research as carefully as the dramatic situation you have found yourself in demands you must.

Once more, let me repeat that there are those, certainly in the major Jewish communities, who have expertise in this area. They can spot the authentic and the fraudulent. The leading rabbi or rabbis of those communities should easily point you in the right direction. At the end of this little book you will find some of their names.

Alternative treatments that may help and do not interfere or disrupt the conventional proven therapies are a useful addition as long as they come with the blessing and endorsement of the doctors and experts dealing with the Big Worry. They should never become replacements for treatments that medical science honestly believes may help.

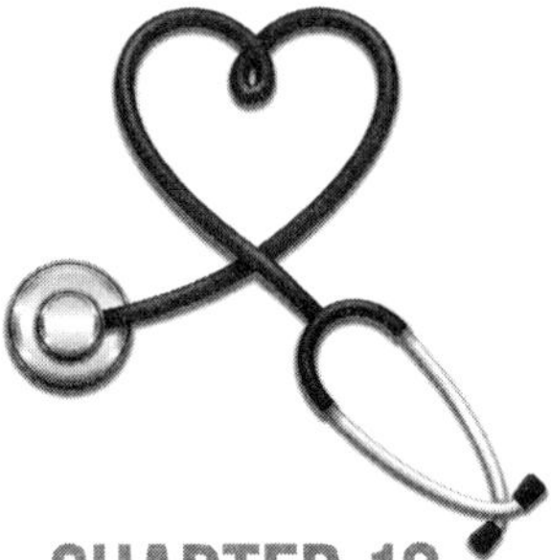

CHAPTER 13

Those Nearest Someone with a Big Worry Have the Big Worry Too

The people nearest to the person with the Big Worry have the Big Worry too. They sometimes need to be handled with the same sensitivity as the person with the illness.

Once again, all the things I mentioned about "equivalence of suffering" and the rest apply to them as well.

Occasionally, people asked me how I was, and I truthfully replied that I was fine. But a little thing — a silly thing — may have distressed me or provoked an angry response, which was totally disproportionate to the incident. That is how I discovered that I was not as "fine" as I'd imagined.

The people closest to the sufferer sometimes can do the greatest kindness by allowing themselves to be shouted at by the sufferer. The friends and family of the ones closest to the sufferer have to allow them to shout sometimes too.

We do not mean to be angry or shout at you. We all call out when we are in pain, even if it achieves nothing. It just demonstrates how much pain we are in.

People nearest to the person with the Big Worry are hurting a lot, even if they themselves don't realize how much pain they are in. They may have been hiding exactly how much pain they are in from others, and from themselves, for a long time. They certainly will have been trying to hide their pain from their children.

Eventually, their pain will surface. They might then become very upset with themselves that they lost control, and let you see how hurt they are.

If you find yourself facing an angry response, it is a huge kindness to let the ones-closest-to-the-sufferer know that you completely understand, and they have nothing whatsoever to apologize for.

People nearest to the person with the Big Worry have the Big Worry too.

> **All the things we mentioned about "equivalence of suffering" and the rest apply to those nearest to someone with a Big Worry as well.**

CHAPTER 14

Seeking the Greatest, Seeking the Wisest

It goes without saying that the very best medical advice and treatment centers should be sought and consulted with when facing a Big Worry. The people mentioned at the end of this book will be able to help you locate and find them. The same holds true for seeking advice from *rabbanim*.

Many years ago, I received a visit from someone I had first met as a young man, who had gone on to become a rabbi. We had remained in touch, and now he had come to seek my advice. He had quite a different kind of Big Worry.

He and his wife were living in Israel, married for a few years, without children. Israel has great expertise in dealing with infertility issues. One of my daughters-in-law is in fact an embryologist in Jerusalem. My sister-in-law works in the same hospital laboratory.

My young friend and his wife had gone for every test available, and all the results pronounced the same verdict. There was simply no possibility that his wife could ever have a baby. They were waiting for the results of one more test, but they had already been told that those results were a foregone conclusion.

The young rabbi felt devastated by his situation, but even more so by incriminating thoughts that sometimes crept into his mind, pointing a finger at his wife and blaming her. "If you had married someone else," a voice said, "you would have had children."

The fact that he could entertain these thoughts, even for a second, disturbed and distressed my friend. He loved his wife and he hated when he heard these words invade his consciousness.

He asked what he should do about them, and I asked him a question. "What makes you so certain that it is your wife's fault? Perhaps the reason she cannot conceive is because Hashem doesn't want *you* to have children.

Whomever you married would have produced the same or a similar situation."

My friend agreed that that made sense. Then I asked him how he knew they could not have children. He explained to me in great detail all of the tests and procedures they had gone through and how every result had confirmed all the others.

"Oh!" I said, "You mean *doctors* have told you that your wife can't have a baby. Have you gone to get a *brachah* from a *tzaddik*?"

He replied that he had been considering doing just that. I told him it would be a "good idea."

On their return to Israel, they went to the doctor who now had the results of the last test he had told me about. He told them precisely what my friend expected him to. "I am afraid the results are exactly as we anticipated," the doctor said. "There is no possibility that your wife will ever become pregnant." He then went on to suggest alternatives, like adoption, that the couple might want to consider.

When he finished, my friend said, "My wife's pregnant." The doctor frowned at the deluded young rabbi who didn't seem to have understood a word he had been saying, so he said them all over again.

Again my friend told him that his wife was expecting a child. The doctor smiled sadly and told him that he had simply made a mistake. They went on to make another five mistakes since that first one. The oldest mistake now has two mistakes of his own.

A *brachah* from a *tzaddik* is not a guarantee, but we know that Heaven is more likely to listen to their requests than an ordinary Jew like me. When combined with the sincere prayers of those suffering from a Big Worry, doctors (who, as I may have mentioned, are only human and make mistakes) are sometimes very pleasantly surprised indeed.

Many years ago, one of my best friends watched his son being wheeled into an operating room for an exploratory operation to determine the cause of his severe stomach problems. The surgeon came out of the room to report the worst news a parent could hear: It was stomach cancer, and he needed an urgent operation to remove the stomach. The father had to give his consent.

My friend was distraught and rushed to ask the Manchester Rosh Yeshivah, Rav Yehudah Zev Segal *zt"l*, what he should do. The *rosh yeshivah* told him that there was nothing to worry about and that everything would be fine. My friend realized that the *rosh yeshivah* hadn't understood that the cancer was already confirmed and they wanted to take out his son's stomach. He repeated in even more distress the situation and again was calmly assured that there was nothing to worry about. Eventually my friend realized the *rosh yeshivah* had understood, and he allowed the surgery to go ahead.

Once more, the same surgeon came out of theater and spoke to my friend. "I have been a surgeon for over twenty years and I know stomach cancer when I see it. It was there yesterday; I don't know what happened, it's completely gone."

I know many such stories. I have been involved in some of them personally. Why a *tzaddik* is able to provoke a positive response from Heaven that no one else can, is not for this book. The truth is, though, that they often can.

There is a story told about a man who had a successful and wonderful life when everything suddenly went wrong. His accountant told him that his business, which had been hugely successful until then, was on the verge of bankruptcy. His daughter told him that she was no longer interested in keeping Torah and *mitzvos*. The man was devastated.

There were two rebbes who lived in his town, and the man sought one out to explain his situation and ask for a *brachah* that everything should be all right. The rebbe listened sympathetically and gave him a warm *brachah*. This made the man feel much better, but as there was another rebbe in town, he decided to go and ask him for a *brachah* too. The second rebbe was as sympathetic as the first and gave an equally warm *brachah*.

The next day, the accountant returned to express his embarrassment and apologies that the information he had delivered the day before had been completely wrong.

There had been a mix-up, and the financial results he had delivered belonged to a different firm altogether. The actual results showed that this had been the man's most successful business year yet! When he returned home to tell his wife the news, he found his daughter in tears, expressing regret that she had even considered deserting her religion. She did not know what had come over her, but now she had returned to her senses and regretted causing her parents any distress.

Then the arguments began. Which rebbe's blessing had produced the miracle? Was it the first rebbe or the second? The followers of each insisted it was their rebbe who had produced the miracle, and as the argument escalated, things become very unpleasant in the town.

Eventually, when things were at their worst and the town divided into two rival camps, one group of Chassidim approached their rebbe and begged him to reveal the truth: Whose blessing had produced the miracle — his, or the other rebbe's?

The rebbe listened, smiled, and then sighed. "Neither rebbe produced the miracle," he replied. "Hashem produced the miracle! The problem is that He doesn't have any Chassidim."

The danger, as the story shows, is that we often forget that ultimately it is Hashem Who cures and removes Big Worries.

There are many stories of Big Worries having happy

endings. Forty percent of cancers are now curable. There is progress in a whole range of conditions and illnesses that were believed to be hopeless not too long ago. There are new therapies that help children with a range of problems that did not exist until recently. Couples who had no hope of having a child a decade ago now have large families.

Although we witness the heroic efforts of doctors and sometimes receive blessings from the greatest of the generation, our challenge is to remember what Hashem Himself tells us in the Torah, "I am Hashem your Doctor." Our challenge is to sincerely tell Him when we pray, that we know it is He Who holds the cure.

There are many, many stories of Big Worries having happy endings. Our challenge is to sincerely tell Hashem when we pray, that we know it is He Who holds the cure.

CHAPTER 15

Sharing News with Wisdom

How much should the children be told when a parent or sibling is seriously ill? That very much depends on the nature of the individual and, of course, their age.

My *rav*, Rabbi Betzalel Rakow *zt"l*, told me that the children should not be told when the situation is "very bad." Years later, I heard of one teenager who has never forgiven her father for not sharing that news. The *rav* had been *niftar* since we spoke about the subject, so I was unable to discuss this with him and ask him to elaborate on a "very bad" situation as it applies to the "worse" situation.

My late mother-in-law *a"h* used to like to quote the Yiddish saying, "*Als ding muz zein mit a mos* — everything should be with a balance."

Of course, we never fail if we ask a *gadol* what we should do. In fact, the more we ask a *gadol*, the less chance we have of erring in judgment.

When our lung specialist pronounced my wife's death sentence, I let my three married sons know relatively quickly, thinking it was only a matter of days until the end. (I assumed that as young men, they no longer fell into the *rav's* definition of children.)

Troubled by the story of the unforgiving teenager, and unsure what my *rav* would have said, I told my unmarried nineteen-year-old son in yeshivah more gradually.

To my thirteen-year-old daughter, I took a different approach. I asked if she was worried about Mummy and she replied that she wasn't. I paused and replied clearly, "I am." That was about as much as I thought appropriate.

I told nothing to my nine-year-old daughter. I didn't feel the *rav's psak* needed any clarification here at all. She knew that Mummy was not well and in the hospital.

I am very glad I didn't tell her any more.

Her mother came home and everything was more or less back to normal. She didn't know how bad things could have been and so this little girl was able to enjoy another half a year worry-free.

To find the missing piece of the advice I could no longer get from my *rav*, I turned to Reb Dovid Cohen *shlit"a*. He told me, unsurprisingly, that there is no set formula, and that what to say and how to say it has to be tailored to each situation and to each child.

Reb Shlomo Brevda *shlit"a* listened to my question with great care and had more specific guidance to offer.

"You should say quite a few *pirkei Tehillim* before you speak to your children, and pray that Hashem should guide your words. Then you should gently and carefully explain to your children that everyone is sent here with a body and a soul for *tikkun*. (Each of us has a unique set of strengths as well as weaknesses. Our job in this world is to promote and perfect those strengths, and channel our weaknesses in a positive direction. That is *tikkun*.)

"You then explain to your children that their parent has managed to perfect and fulfill the task he or she was sent here for earlier than most people, and Hashem is calling their *neshamah* home again. We should say that of course, we — who love them — are heartbroken and sad. The Ramban says that when someone we love is leaving to move to another place we are sad. Leaving this world for the next is no different. We will, though, see them again very soon." Then Rabbi Brevda said, "You take your children and hug them very close. The last thing to tell them is that every good thing that we as children and family do now, will have a very, very far-reaching effect on that *neshamah* that we love so much, in *Shamayim*."

Professionals in this field assure me that the children must be prepared. Our *gedolim* can help us judge how and when.

I often point out to people who have just lost a loved one that time as we understand and experience it only applies in this world. It does not exist in heaven.

When someone closes his eyes here for the last time, surrounded by his family, he opens them again immediately in heaven to find himself surrounded by exactly the same people he just "left behind." Even though we remain behind down here to complete our own lives and *tikkun*, in heaven's terms — where our concept of time does not apply — we have already lived our lives and have come back again! We are already there, and when our loved one — a parent, a brother, sister or child — opens his or her eyes, those who surrounded them seconds before with tear-filled eyes surround them again with warm, loving smiles and laughter.

How much children should be told has to be guided by *daas Torah*.

CHAPTER 16

Afterward

I remember once visiting the *rav* of Gateshead, Rabbi Betzalel Rakow *zt"l*.

We were shmoozing together, and in the course of the conversation he mentioned that one of the stalwarts of the community, whom I knew well, had passed away. I had not heard this news and was both surprised and shocked. The *rav* saw my surprise and when I asked him, "How old was he?" he smiled and said pensively, "How old was he?" He paused and looked at me wisely and said, "He was precisely the age when *Hashem Yisbarach* wanted his *neshamah* back again!"

Yaffa was ill for five years before she reached precisely

the age when *Hashem Yisbarach* wanted her *neshamah* back again. I was with her when He did. Our doctor and friend had provided every possible comfort and she passed away peacefully and quietly at home, surrounded by her family.

If this were to be a much bigger work, I could tell you more of the details of those five years. There were many times for tears but much, much laughter too. We saw and discovered the very best in people we thought we knew. We saw and discovered the very best in ourselves and our children.

In fact, we found the lump a year before it was diagnosed. A doctor simply misdiagnosed it and thought it was nothing to worry about. If he hadn't, then I would probably not be writing this book.

Doctors are human and, like every one of us, make mistakes. If I make an error as a rabbi, you might come to eat something which I mistakenly thought was kosher when in fact it wasn't.

If a doctor makes a mistake, then something he thinks is nothing to worry about instead turns into a Big Worry. I bear no ill feelings over this. I could only do so if I never made mistakes myself, and after all, Yaffa was ill for five years until precisely the age when *Hashem Yisbarach* wanted her *neshamah* back again.

She passed away just before Shavuos, and a few of my best friends in London wanted to send me and my family away to Switzerland after we got up from *shivah*. I was reluctant to accept their kindness, but was eventually persuaded that it was the best thing to do.

We arrived in a mountain village called Flims a few hours before Shavuos began, and as we were all tired from the flight, we went for a nap. Yaffa came to me in a dream.

I don't know if you have ever had this experience, although of course the *sefarim* talk about it in many places. It is a completely different phenomenon to an ordinary dream in every way.

She was smiling at me warmly and I asked, "How come you are here?" She did not reply but simply continued to smile. Then I found I was awake. I was so annoyed I had woken up and tried to fall asleep immediately so I could ask her things and speak to her, but I simply couldn't fall back asleep. I knew, though, that she had come back for those few moments just to let me know that she was all right and happy, now that the difficult times were past.

I was reluctant to write this here. Perhaps, despite my very real conviction that this dream was so very different and that Yaffa *had* appeared to let me know she was okay, I was wrong. Perhaps after all, it was just a dream.

When I shared this story with Rabbi Brevda *shlit"a*, I said perhaps I was being ridiculous and had imagined the whole thing. He told me that I was not being ridiculous at all and that it was very likely indeed to have been as I told him — a brief visit to let me know I could stop worrying, and as her *neshamah's tikkun* was complete, everything was now fine.

> **People are at precisely the right age when *Hashem Yisbarach* wants their *neshamos* back again!**

CHAPTER 17

Why Do Very Bad Things Happen to Very Good People?

I recall a very good friend of mine, who is a rabbi in Livingston, New Jersey, telling me of the most distressing incident in his ten-year-old daughter's life. One of her classmates' mothers got sick. The entire class poured out their hearts in prayer. They took on extra *mitzvos* and *chessed* in the *zechus* of the mom. Despite all the prayers and all their efforts, she passed away.

"I don't understand," my friend's daughter asked her

daddy. "We prayed so hard, but Hashem didn't answer our prayers!"

The rabbi looked down at the tear-filled eyes of his little girl and said, "You are quite wrong, you know. He did answer your prayers. The answer was 'no'!"

That answer may have been too hard for a little girl. It is hard enough for grown men and women.

Even Moshe Rabbeinu struggled with it. He saw Jewish children's bodies used to fill gaps in the buildings their parents were being forced to build for Pharaoh in Egypt. Moshe begged Hashem to put a stop to the carnage. Why do bad things happen to really good people?

When my late wife *a"h* and I used to travel to the Christie at times when remaining optimistic was very difficult, there was a sign we had to pass which made our suffering pale by comparison. It read, "Young Oncology Unit."

Schoolchildren notice a friend has been away for too long and are baffled to see them return much thinner and with all their hair gone. Babies are born dead, and babies go to sleep never to wake up. Famous *baalei tzedakah* lose their wealth. A golden young couple who celebrated the wedding of the year finds themselves standing in front of a *beis din* a year later while a *sofer* finishes writing a *get*.

Why do terrible things happen to really good people?

At the end of *Parshas Shemos* (5:22), Moshe returned

to Hashem, Who had sent him on a mission. The mission had failed and Moshe issued an accusation.

"*Lamah harei'osah l'am hazeh...* — 'Why have You done bad to this people?' Why have You sent me? From the time You sent me to Pharaoh to speak in Your Name it has been evil for this people and You have not rescued Your people!"

Reb Simcha Zissel *zt"l* explains that Moshe was so at one with his people that he was only expressing how *they* were feeling after his failure.

Still, in this story is mapped out the normal human reaction to suffering and pain, "Why?"

We want to know why this has happened and we want to know now.

Hashem's answer is contained in the next verse... *"Now you will see what I will do to Pharaoh!"*

We want the answer to "Why?" — to the young mother who succumbed to cancer, or the baby who failed to wake up — that will take away, or at least explain, our pain. Hashem's answer is: You will have to wait to find it. (At times of pain like these, we forget about all of the babies that do wake up every morning and the people who are treated and cured of cancer.)

The midrash says that Moshe saw an image of Hashem on Mount Sinai. He was wearing *tefillin*. Moshe saw the knot of Hashem's *tefillin*. As the Biala Rebbe writes, you can usually only see Hashem from behind...when you look back.

I wrote in my book, *Dancing Through Time,* about an episode that occurred during World War II.

During the 1930s, the trickle of Jews fleeing Germany turned into a flood. According to the famous English writer George Orwell, there was almost as much anti-Semitism in the UK before the war as there was in Germany.

In general, the British only opened their doors to refugees who possessed skills the country could use, such as doctors, dentists, etc., and refugees were known by the pejorative nickname, "refu-Jews!"

When war broke out, thousands of such Jews became officially categorized as "enemy aliens." The government had them temporarily shipped off to the Isle of Man, off of England's west coast. Eventually it was decided to send them to Australia.

England was losing thousands of tons of its merchant fleet every week to German U-boat packs, and vessels and sailors were very precious. A ship was eventually found to bring the refugees to Australia. It was called the *Dunera.*

Finding a crew proved more difficult. If so many ships were being sunk, many sailors were losing their lives. Someone came up with an unusual idea.

England's prisons contained lots of sailors. Some of them had committed terrible crimes, and their sentences were very long. If they would volunteer to crew the

Dunera, they might receive a pardon. This was promptly arranged, and those poor Jewish souls, many of whom had lost wives and children, set sail for Australia.

A few days into the voyage, the crew went berserk and robbed their passengers of everything they possessed. Watches and jewelry were ripped from terrified hands. Suitcases were ransacked and valuables stolen, and the rest was thrown into the sea. These Jews, who had already suffered so much, were left with nothing in the world other than the clothes on their backs.

One can easily imagine the anguish and frustration they must have felt as they stood at the foot of the gangplank, having finally arrived in Australia. After all that has happened to us, why did Hashem have to allow that, too? You can easily imagine them calling out to Heaven, "*Lamah harei'osah l'am hazeh* — Why have You done bad to this people?"

It took many years for that question to be answered. Someone was browsing at a book stall in a flea market in Amsterdam when he discovered and purchased the journal of a U-boat captain.

The submariner recounted that one day, he was sailing underwater in the Atlantic when he ordered the periscope raised. As he gazed through the eyepiece, he saw a British merchant ship on the horizon. It was the *Dunera.*

Swiveling the periscope 360 degrees, he discovered no

escorting warships. This was a plump and easy target.

He ordered a torpedo fired at the ship, but after a few seconds there was no sound of an explosion. The torpedo seemed to have missed.

He raised the periscope a second time to take new bearings, and indeed the ship was sailing along, ignorant of the fact that it was under attack or that the ominous wake of a torpedo's propeller was cutting a white path in the sea just behind the ship.

Then the captain became confused. Floating in the water was lots of debris. He could see suitcases bobbing up and down. That is what he often saw after he had hit a ship. What was debris doing there when he hadn't?

He ordered the U-boat to the surface, and some of his crew grabbed pieces of the floating luggage. This was taken below and opened.

The Nazi sailors were horrified to see what was inside. Among assorted clothes were books — German books! German Jews read German books, Goethe and Kant and others. The German captain, though, came to a different conclusion. This ship was carrying German prisoners of war!

The captain radioed back to the German admiralty to relay what he had discovered and received an order to escort the *Dunera* on its journey to Australia. It should also signal to other Axis submarines not to attack.

I told this story in a *shiur* in yeshivah recently, and one of my *talmidim* told me his grandfather had been on the *Dunera*. It was the culmination of a flight from Germany to England and then imprisonment. Despite the fact that he neither wanted to be there nor understood why he was there, he carried on as a Jew must — even still. A long time would have to pass before he could see that what looked like the final straw — the final indignity of losing his precious, last possessions — was exactly what Hashem had designed to save his life. Eventually Hashem would allow him to see and understand that this had been part of His plan.

We want to know now why terrible things are happening to us or those we love. Hashem says we will usually have to wait to find out.

I recall another incident that occurred in Amsterdam, this time to me.

I was attending the wedding of a *talmid*, and as I sat at the "rabbis" table, someone whom I had not seen for a long time came in and sat down beside me.

After we exchanged "*Shalom Aleichems*," he surprised me with a startling statement, "I have big *tainahs* (complaints) against the Gateshead yeshivah!" We had both learned there. He continued, "Why didn't they warn us what happens after you leave yeshivah?"

I listened as he explained that after he left Gateshead, he had gone to learn in a *kollel*. It was a community *kollel*, constructed in such a way that the members devoted a large part of their time to learning with the local residents who wanted to discover more about their Jewish heritage.

In choosing to learn there, he thought he was doing a good — even noble — thing, and thus was shocked to discover that there were many in his new town who did not share his viewpoint. Opposition came even from a rabbi or two, who had once been enthusiastic and idealistic like himself, but who had settled into a comfortable lifestyle where they had grown too much like the congregants who should have grown to be like them.

I smiled. I, too, had gone to such a *kollel* and I, too, had high hopes of playing a positive role and helping many Jews. These hopes were in fact realized, but I, too, found that many people in the town disliked me intensely for my efforts, including, sadly, one or two who had also learned in yeshivah.

I turned to my friend and explained that I had shared his experience. I had even had the same *tainah*, but only for a little while. When I did, a voice inside my head asked me a simple question: "Yehudah Yonah: In those seven years that you were in Gateshead Yeshivah, did you never once attend a *Chumash shiur*? Did you never ever go to a *mussar shmuess* (ethical discourse)?

"Did Avraham have an easy life? How about Yitzchak, or let's think about Yaakov Avinu and his life.

"His brother fought with him in the womb. He fought

with him after they were born. His mother instructed him to oppose his given nature which yearned for truth and honesty and turn himself into a fraud by pretending to be Eisav and take his blessing. Then Yaakov had to flee from his brother's vengeance and he nearly lost his life again.

"He carries out his parents' wishes and goes to marry his *bashert* (destined one), only to find himself cheated of his bride, and the possessor of the father-in-law from Gehinnom! Together with his family, he has to flee from this father-in-law who seeks to catch up with him and kill him. Eventually he comes to the land of Israel.

"There, his brother Eisav, who has been nursing his anger all the years of his absence, attempts to kill him again.

"Peace at last comes to Yaakov in the Holy Land. Then his daughter is raped and kidnapped. His sons Shimon and Levi exact a revenge that Yaakov feels is wrong and again his life and that of his children are in jeopardy.

"At last the family settles down to normalcy and spiritual growth when the son, who is the apple of his eye, disappears — either kidnapped or killed. Yaakov Avinu is plunged into despair and consequently loses prophecy. Did Yaakov Avinu have an easy life?"

The problem was that of course I went to *shiurim* where these incidents were delved into. I understood the deep insights that were revealed. I just missed the fact that they applied to me. The lessons of the *Avos* and how they dealt with crises and disasters apply to every age and to everyone, you and me. How Avraham dealt with his problems and how Sarah dealt with hers is the model of how we should deal with ours. It wasn't what happened *then*; it's what should happen *now*.

Rav Samson Raphael Hirsch *zt"l* asks a question about Yaakov Avinu based on the first verse in the last *sedra* in *Bereishis*. The *pasuk* says:

> *And Yaakov lived in Egypt seventeen years, and it was that the days of Yaakov, the years of his life, were one hundred and forty-seven years.*

"What," asks Rav Hirsch, "was the best part of Yaakov Avinu's life? Was it the first 130 years, or the last seventeen years when the family was reunited in an exclusively Jewish enclave of Egypt? *Yeshivos* had been established by Yehudah. Yaakov was reunited with his beloved son Yosef!"

The obvious answer is the last seventeen years.

But in which part of his life did he achieve greatness to such an extent that Hashem changed his name from Yaakov to one that denoted a far higher spiritual level, to Yisrael? That occurred in the first 130 years of conflict, flight, pain, and loss.

None of the *Avos* had things easy. Avraham came from a home which today would be described by sociologists as "dysfunctional." So did Sarah, Rivkah, Rachel, and Leah. They all had fathers and siblings who, at best, were failed human beings. They all rejected their unsavory origins and achieved greatness. A person is not condemned by a tough background.

I once heard Rebbetzin Heller of Jerusalem explain an astounding idea. She pointed out that the Rambam talks about four levels of suffering.

The first level of suffering is financial suffering. The second level is worse — ill health. The third, even worse level — vicarious suffering, where you suffer for someone else, like the parents of the children who have to follow the sign that says "Young Oncology Unit." The last and the worst level of suffering is — no suffering!

Let's consider the words of the Rambam.

Imagine someone who is incredibly wealthy and loses everything overnight. I know people like that. Once, walking along a street in Chicago, a man approached me with a request, "Could you spare me ten dollars for my medications?"

I produced a ten-dollar bill and handed it to the man. "Thanks!" he said. "Do you know of a Chabad House I could go to for a meal?" I told him that I had passed one two blocks down and he thanked me and went on his way. After I had taken a few steps, he called out to me, "You know, I used to be a millionaire!"

What are the negative reactions that a person might

have to having lost everything and plunging from material security to begging to be given ten dollars for medication?

The obvious ones are despair and depression. Then there will be anger with himself and others. There may even be anger with G-d. There will also be embarrassment and shame. His self-esteem may be shattered; self-pity may take over.

Now consider what positive reactions he might have to losing all his money. This question might strike you as strange. Positive reactions to this? Think about it; there could be many.

He might find himself in sympathy with people whose struggles and worries he had no notion of before. He might discover a question that could not be answered before now: "Who are my real friends?" It may bring him closer to G-d. It may be a humbling experience that he uses to discover strengths in his character he didn't know were there.

Who chooses how we react to circumstances of financial hardship, either positively or negatively? We do.

Now imagine someone who was healthy, vigorous, and fit. One day this man is struck by an illness which requires major surgery and long-term rehabilitation.

What are the negative reactions that a person might have to having lost his health?

The previous list applies here too, but as this is more

serious and dramatic, the list is longer. There will be fear that the treatment will not work. There will be fear of pain and dying. There may be the humiliation of not being able to perform even the simplest tasks of personal hygiene.

Now consider what positive reactions he might have to having lost his health.

Again, all the previous positive reactions apply here too.

If you have ever suffered ill health or been close to someone who has, you will know that life becomes serious and real. There is often the realization that ninety percent of what most of us concern ourselves with and struggle for is total nonsense. Did you get the latest iPhone or the current season's designer clothes? New cars do not secure happiness, and only the shallowest person will assess the value of a person's life in terms of his material possessions.

Soon after my late wife received her diagnosis, I recall coming home from shul on Shabbos morning. I passed by a house where a young father was standing in the doorway with his baby in his arms. He was shouting in anger at his wife. I do not know what he said or what the fight was about. I only remember thinking to myself, "It doesn't matter... It really doesn't matter!"

My good friend Jonathan Rosenblum once told me a story about a doctor, who shares my surname, who had fought for and saved a woman's life when the other doctors had given up. When he entered the room the next day to visit the patient, he found her husband beside her bed. He leaped to his feet and declared, "That's him! That's the doctor who wouldn't give up!"

The woman said, "I'm not going to thank you, Dr. Rubinstein. But when I get home to my own bed and wake up to hear the birds singing in the branches on the tree outside my window, I'm going to say, 'Thank you, Dr. Rubinstein.' And when I take my little girl in my arms for the first time, I'm going to say, 'Thank you, Dr. Rubinstein.' And when I am well enough to take her to school and pick her up to bring her home again, I'm going to say, 'Thank you, Dr. Rubinstein.'"

Who will choose how we react to illness, either positively or negatively? Again, we do.

Now imagine a mother and a father who have a seriously ill child. The child may have developed the illness or he may have been born ill.

The negative reactions here are very dramatic. The child's condition could drive the parents to reject the child. This is particularly true if the condition affects the child's intellectual abilities, like Down Syndrome or autism. It might drive the parents to reject each other. If the condition was caused by a flawed gene passed by either the mother or the father, the one who does not suffer from the defect might blame the one who does.

Anger, depression, despair, and all the others might be felt at a very intense level.

The positive reactions are almost a mirror image of the negative. The child's illness may bring the mother and father closer than any normal couple will ever be. It might bring the couple closer to the child than any normal parents might be to an ordinary child. The charities that combat childhood disease are almost always set up by parents whose child or children have suffered the same childhood disease.

Here too, at this most intense level, we will choose whether we become negative or positive in this situation. We will choose to become better or bitter. The difference between the two is "I."

That was not, though, the Rambam's worst level of suffering. He reserved that for those who experience no suffering!

Everyone is born with certain weaknesses in their personalities, and certain strengths. As we move through life we are supposed work to promote the strengths and demote the weaknesses.

There are some, though, who simply do not find it within themselves to change their behavior. Seeing that such people cannot generate change from within, it's possible they need help to change from the outside. (There are many other explanations in the words of *Chazal* on why people suffer, when the person suffering has done nothing to deserve the situation.)

Such a person may have to go through a period of financial hardship or ill health or even the pain of seeing someone they love suffer. From all of these experiences, we agreed previously that they can choose the positive, and grow and improve *because* of that suffering.

There are, though, some people who are incapable of choosing positively. No matter what happens to them, they will not choose better, only bitter. Such people may indeed experience carefree, untroubled lives.

G-d does not make people suffer for the sake of inflicting pain. If He sees there is no possibility of good being chosen through difficult times, why send them? Let such a person "have it all" down here. He is certainly not going to have it in the Next World. (Once again, that does not mean that everyone who has an easy life is a write-off" — we can't possibly figure out all of Hashem's calculations.)

Suffering can be a second chance — an opportunity — to change that which you would not have found without suffering.

Rav Dessler explains it by pointing to the Hebrew word for evil or bad — *ra*. If you ask anyone what is the opposite of *ra*, they will answer, *tov* (good).

Rav Dessler answers that the opposite of *ra* — spelled *resh, ayin* — is actually the Hebrew word *er*, spelled *ayin, resh*. This word means "awake" or "catalyst."

The statistics make it clear that alcoholics go on to raise children who often become alcoholics. Many child abusers were abused as children, and bullies bring up bullies. But it doesn't have to be like that. Let me repeat that, IT DOESN'T HAVE TO BE LIKE THAT!

The opposite of *ra* is *er*.

Rav Dessler gives four examples.

In the Haggadah we say, *In the beginning our forefathers were idolaters, Terach was the father of Avraham*. Why trace our lineage back beyond Avraham to his father? Avraham was the first Jew, not Terach.

When Hashem prepared the Jewish people for the giving of the Torah at Sinai, where did that preparation take place? In Jerusalem, Lakewood, or Gateshead?

It was of course in Egypt, a bloody exile where two thousand Jewish babies were slaughtered day and night. Pharaoh wanted their blood, which he imagined would cure him of his leprosy.

Consider where the greatest Jew who ever lived — Moshe — had his upbringing.

It was not in a *cheder* or yeshivah in Eretz Yisrael, but instead he was bounced on the knee of a man who believed himself to be a god.

Lastly, Rav Dessler points to Rus, the grandmother of Dovid Hamelech and Mashiach.

Rus came from Moav, a nation known in *Chazal* as "*ha'umah hab'zuyah* — the most disgusting of all the peoples." They originated from an act of incest (with Lot and his daughters) and boasted of it in their name Moav, which means "from my father."

If Hashem was looking for a young woman to carry the seed of the Mashiach in her womb, might He not have looked instead to some nice Jewish girl who lived in Bnei Brak?

The answer to all of these puzzles is the same. The opposite of *ra* is *er*.

It was precisely because Avraham had a father who was one of the leading proponents of idolatry in his time that caused him to steer his life in exactly the opposite direction and discover the real G-d.

It was the 210 years that the Jewish people endured the evil of Egypt that caused them to wake up and reject it. That rejection led them to Mount Sinai.

Being bounced on the knee of someone who thought himself a god caused Moshe Rabbeinu to look for and come face to face with Hashem.

It was exactly because Rus came from the nation which boasted of their immorality that was the catalyst for her to reject it. She went on to become the paradigm of female modesty. That's why when she bent to pick up the fallen grain in the field, she bent in such a way that her skirts covered her legs. She had learned well the lessons of Moav, and then rejected them totally.

It is true that alcoholics produce children who become

alcoholics. Many child abusers were abused as children and bullies bring up bullies.

BUT IT DOESN'T HAVE TO BE LIKE THAT! The opposite of *ra* is *er*.

A few years ago I was a "Scholar-in-Residence" at a *Shabbaton* in San Diego. One of my lectures was based on these ideas. At Shabbos lunch I was approached by someone who had been listening to me and who told me that he was scheduled to speak at the *seudah shlishis*, which he was sponsoring. He said, "Rabbi, you've taken away everything I wanted to say! I was in Auschwitz and I am speaking later on."

I wanted to hear, though, what an Auschwitz survivor would have to say on the subject of suffering.

He began with a story. "One day a bunch of us boys were standing at the corner of one of the barracks within sight of the chimneys of the crematoria. One of the boys said, 'I'm happy I'm in Auschwitz!'

"We looked at him and asked, 'What did you say?'

"He repeated, 'I'm happy I'm in Auschwitz!'

"We shouted at him, 'Are you crazy?! Are you *meshugah*?!'

"He smiled and replied, 'No, I'm not *meshugah*. And if I wasn't happy, so where would I be? Still in Auschwitz!'"

I sat there with my jaw agape as he continued.

"The Gemara talks about someone called Nachum Ish Gamzu. Whatever happened to him in his life, he always said, '*Gam zu l'tovah* — This is also for the good!'"

Then this survivor turned to his audience of four hundred or so and asked, "Do you know how you read that Gemara? '*Gam zu... l'tovah*! Also this, I will make good!'"

Then he addressed his final words to his audience.

"And if you haven't suffered, you haven't lived! If you haven't suffered, YOU'RE NOTHING! Because how else are you going to help someone when they're suffering?"

We choose to become either better or bitter. The difference between the two is 'I.'

CHAPTER 18

Conclusion

Lo al yedei bizayon v'lo al yedei nisayon — "Not through embarrassment nor through tests."

No one volunteers for tests and challenges. In fact, we pray every morning that we shouldn't be tested or challenged. I have said these words and the words from the previous chapters in lectures all over the world. Dealing with serious illness has been and is one of my most important talks. In fact, five Holocaust survivors who have heard it told me that they agree with my perspective on this subject. Those are precious endorsements indeed.

In addition, after I gave this talk a few years ago at

a *Shabbaton* in Toronto, many people stayed to ask further questions on this subject; all were either cancer patients or spouses of cancer patients. They knew that I understood what they were going through, and that I had an equivalence of suffering. They wanted my advice, and I was glad that I could provide it. Certainly I would have never volunteered for the experiences that equipped me to give such advice. Rather, I would have volunteered *not* to have those experiences.

While one person's Big Worry might be the struggle to bring a child into this world, another fears he will watch one leave it. Many may face illness, surgery, or anything else we have mentioned in the previous chapters. There are few of us though, if any, who haven't suffered at one time or another. Yet we learn that through this suffering one can grow and thus be equipped to help others when they are suffering. Often those who have dealt with or are dealing with a Big Worry have a much clearer view of this world than the rest of us.

Rav Dessler writes about someone who has *ruach hakodesh* (Divine inspiration) and how he sees things differently too.

"They see the true essence and value of everything from inanimate objects to people. They understand the spiritual worth of things too. They comprehend the part everything plays in the structure and purpose of the world... There is a purity that means that when their mind sees the truth, it

is not distorted by their own wants and desires."

I think that is often why those who are seriously ill seem to have an understanding, wisdom, and calmness about their situation that others find — to say the least — surprising. Allow me to explain what I mean.

A few years ago, on the first night of Pesach, I ran a communal Seder for Gateways at a hotel in Stamford, Connecticut. Halfway through the Seder, one of the ninety or so participants stood up and asked if he could say something. I was happy to rest my voice and warmly welcomed what I assumed would be a *dvar Torah*. When this thirty-something-year-old young man started to speak, I misheard and misunderstood what he was saying.

He explained that he should not actually be with us at the hotel at all. He was scheduled to be in the hospital and I thought he meant that he was a doctor who should have been working over the holiday. In fact, he meant that he should have been having treatment but that his appointment had been delayed.

He pointed and smiled at his smartly dressed wife who sat beside him. She smiled back and he continued, "Two years ago my wife was diagnosed with a brain tumor." The participants at the Seder became totally silent as he went on, "The doctor delivering the diagnosis told us, 'Don't worry — it could be worse, it could be cancer!'" Everyone was riveted by his words and he carried on.

"She had an operation and follow-up treatment, and

a year later she was healthy. We went to see the same doctor for the results of tests that I was having and as we sat before him, he told me *I* had cancer."

At these words we were all both stunned and shocked. He looked us with a smile on his lips and in his eyes and said, "The doctor then told us, 'Don't worry — it could be worse...it could be a brain tumor!'"

The young man and his wife reminded him what he had said when he delivered her diagnosis twelve months before and the doctor said, "Ouch! I think I will have to get some new lines," and all three of them laughed.

He, too, completed his treatment and although there was still a little more to do, he assured us that both of them were now well.

With the insertion of this note of humor, he then pointed to the Haggadah and the words we had reached before he had asked to speak.

Therefore we are obliged to give thanks, praise, and honor...to Hashem, Who has done for our forefathers and for us, all of these miracles.

He repeated those words slowly and concluded by telling us, "You should know that what is written here is absolutely true. What Hashem does is all good...*all* of it, even if we don't understand. We have to thank Hashem!" With his wife nodding in agreement, he sat down.

That was how they really saw what had happened to them. They were one hundred percent sincere and convinced about this. They saw things differently than other people. I thought it was akin to *ruach hakodesh.* Their perspective was calm and happy and comprehending.

Two years later, they invited my wife and me to their son's bar mitzvah in New Jersey. Unfortunately, we weren't able to join them, but we, along with all who could come, knew that this special *simchah* celebrated not just a young man's entry into adulthood, but a family whose perspective was, *Ani Hashem rofecha* — "I am Hashem, your Doctor."

CHAPTER 19

A British Doctor's View

Dr. David Landau is the Consultant Oncologist at Guys & St. Thomas Hospital and London Oncology Clinic, in London, UK.

Rabbi Rubinstein's book gives people who have received a potentially devastating piece of news the opportunity to regain their spiritual poise and control of their lives. I am grateful for the opportunity to add some further thoughts on the same theme from my experiences as a practising oncologist.

I believe strongly that patients need to engage meaningfully in the fight against their illness.

Why?

There is no doubt in my mind that patients who give up and decide that their situation is hopeless, fare less well. This may be because they are, to an extent, depressed, and depression is in itself a negative factor. It is also likely that if a patient has a positive outlook and a feeling that he or she is fighting usefully to beat the illness, then the treatment is more effective and in some way, the outcome is improved. This is not a very mainstream perspective and is not based on solid scientific evidence. Different degrees of positive and negative are not possible to measure. It has, however, been shown in observational clinical trials that patients with depression or similar, have a worse outcome. That a positive attitude improves outcomes has not been shown in clinical trials but in my and many others' experience, it is true.

It is also true, I believe, that a patient's response to treatment side effects is impacted by their engagement in the fight. Accepting side effects as part of an active struggle is perhaps more acceptable and less demoralising than experiencing them as part of an inevitable and uncontrollable nightmare.

How can one engage in the fight?

All individuals must choose for themselves how they are going to fight their illnesses. For some it is the way they live their life, and for others it is in the treatments they choose to receive.

I recall one gentleman well into his eighties, who refused to change his lifestyle one jot. He was a famous philanthropist and spent his time visiting the many institutions he supported. He enjoyed having lunch or dinner with his friends and associates and would work his chemotherapy schedule entirely around his pre-existing social calendar. If one treatment was not working, he would immediately say, "So, David, what do we do next?" There was no question of allowing the illness to control his life. The same philosophy can be taken in so many different ways. Not to miss a *tefillah,* to always be in control of one's behaviour toward others, to always buy chocolates for the nurses, or not to stop a *daf yomi* (daily folio of Talmud) or *shemiras halashon* (proper speech) programme. The key is to set your own agenda and not allow it to be dictated by the illness.

Other patients begin on a quest for the best possible treatment. In many situations, this is not actually necessary in order to ensure that the best treatment is given. The rigour with which most standard therapies has been established means that many good options already exist and will be offered to the patient by their team of specialists. One patient of mine, though, has a rare type of cancer for which the recognised options are few. He scours the Internet and is in touch with top academic centres around the world to try to identify promising clinical trials into which he might enrol. It is worth pointing out, too, that he has adopted one particular doctor in his team with whom he talks through his research findings, and does not travel abroad for treatment unless he is clear what he is travelling for. He tries as far as possible to have any treatment locally. Many other patients achieve the same without the same degree of effort. Many put themselves wholeheartedly into the prescribed treatment offered to them by their team whilst others find a complementary therapy or medication that suits them and allows them to make their own contribution to their treatment.

The key I suggest is to think through — with the help of one's family or friends — exactly what one wishes one's attitude to be and not to just let events take over. In this way, individual decisions and reactions form part of an overall picture that might just make a little more sense. The feeling that events are spiralling out of control is unfortunately all too common, and can soon give way to feelings of depression and despair. If someone is truly engaged in the fight against the illness, I believe that this is less likely.

What is a normal reaction to receiving bad news?

It is not easy for doctors to give bad news, but it is always so much more difficult for the patient and their relatives and friends to receive it. Not all doctors deliver bad news as effectively or sensitively as others, and this can clearly impact the reaction the patient has to receiving the news. Nevertheless, there are other factors that contribute toward clarifying patients' different reactions. These might include events from childhood through adulthood, or past experiences to current conceptions (or misconceptions). Regardless of these factors, it is difficult to think of an abnormal reaction. All reactions are normal and therefore reasonable and acceptable.

How does a *frum* Jew react?

We are all human beings with a history of personal experiences and emotions and these will overwhelmingly shape and define our reactions, particularly in the immediate aftermath of receiving bad news. There are some very special people who are able to react naturally with pure Torah character. For most of us, though, it is unrealistic to expect that our instinctive and on-the-spot reactions should be quite so refined. Subsequently, however, we are obliged to reflect on our situations from a Torah perspective. This does not mean that we will not be at all upset, angry, disappointed or even self-conscious. It does not imply that we give up the fight. It certainly does not suggest that we understand why we have been put in this situation. It will signify something different to each of us and that is important — not just for the patient, but for the relatives as well.

How can one make receiving bad news less stressful?

It is always a good idea for someone to accompany the patient when any news might be given, because apart from having to listen to all the information that is imparted, the message needs to be digested and coped with, and a second pair of ears is likely to be very helpful.

What help is available?

In England we are blessed in that most Orthodox Jews are members of real communities with a *rav* who is often the first port of call in times of need. Apart from helping one to try and see things from a Torah perspective, the *rav* is also likely to have had some relevant experience and may also be able to offer some practical help.

We also have both formal and informal support systems. The Chai Lifeline organization, for example, has offices in London and Manchester. There are many other groups — some more and some less formal — that can be accessed through local *rabbanim*, that are often very useful. These bodies should not be seen as helpful only to those who cannot help themselves; they have something significant to offer most cancer sufferers and I encourage all patients to consider contacting them.

What about clinical trials?

There are a few common attitudes to clinical trials. One is, "I don't want to be a guinea pig." Another is, "If it's a new drug in a trial, that means they think it could be the next big thing. I want it." Which is the correct view?

There are halachic aspects to clinical trials that I am not qualified to comment on. It is extremely important, though, to understand the context of clinical trials. Before any drug can be licensed, it must be tested in clinical trials. Therefore, almost all drugs that are currently used in standard practice have been through clinical trials. Most drugs going through the clinical trials process are not successful — that is, they are not ultimately found to be any better than the current standard treatment. Therefore, starting with standard treatments makes sense because they are the successful drugs of the last generation of clinical trials performed in recent years.

There are, sometimes, new drugs that look very promising, but do not yet have a license for various reasons. In this scenario, a clinical trial might be the best way to access the drug.

All drugs must also be tested for safety, and this is usually performed before there is any data on the effectiveness of the drug. In this situation, one must carefully weigh the likely risks and benefits of joining the study. Increasingly, even these early clinical trials are focusing as much as possible on patients who might be expected to have some useful clinical response from the drugs. The main point is that there are many different types of clinical trials, and one must take this into account in one's decision making.

As a doctor, I will, of course, finish by saying that one should maintain a friendly and open relationship with the treating team. Communication is always key to a good relationship and this is no different. Always mention what is troubling you. Write down questions so you don't forget them during a consultation. Show your appreciation and usually the feelings will be reciprocated.

CHAPTER 20

An Israeli Doctor's View

Dr. Andrew Fink is a Consultant Ophthalmologist in Ra'anana, Israel.

My father was eighty-six when he died. Three years previously, he'd fallen down the stairs, and although he hadn't sustained any serious injury, we could pinpoint his slow deterioration in health to that moment. He was in and out of the hospital on numerous occasions during this time, suffering various ailments common to old age, none of which were fatal. Each time he would come home, better than when he went into the hospital, but not quite as well as after his previous discharge. Gradually, he lost weight and his mobility, and we were eventually compelled to find him a rest home for full-time nursing care. This would be his final "station" during his long and active life.

We decided not to tell Dad that from this admission he would not be coming home. We were sure he'd cope better, feeling he was just in for temporary assessment and treatment, like his many other hospital admissions. However, he also never asked, so we didn't have to face the dilemma of how to tell him.

One morning, a consultant physician visited and whether Dad asked him, we're not sure. However, a conversation developed, the result of which was that Dad understood he would never be going home. He was in for terminal nursing care. The physician had acted correctly according to the law. The patient has the right to know. However, the physician hadn't previously consulted with us — his family — about how to convey the information, and as became apparent, hadn't left any element of hope in his explanation.

Dad was stunned when we next spoke to him, and clearly had genuinely not realized how ill he was, or was simply in denial. His morale plummeted, and despite our efforts to undo the psychological damage, he never really recovered his optimistic spirit during the remaining weeks of his life.

These events could have happened anywhere in the world, even with the best planning in advance. Managing the Big Worry is an issue faced by medical caretakers, patients, and their close ones every day in many different situations. It may be tempting to hide the truth from a sick relative sometimes, especially if it is felt by those close to the patient that the psychological harm will be excessive. There are situations where the importance of maintaining life and preventing discomfort is more important than the absolute truth. Those who know the patient well may feel the truth will lead to despair or even suicidal thoughts. A parent may have made a specific request to his children years previously that he doesn't want to know the truth, preferring to fade away peacefully. If no treatment is available and the cooperation of the patient for complicated procedures is not required, this course of action may well be valid sometimes.

However, in most cases in Israel, the patient is told the whole truth. In my experience, after the initial shock, people feel relief at having the uncertainty removed. With the help of the modern media, patients have often researched their disease, and clarification often helps to counter the partial information or confused understanding acquired from a Google search.

Relationships between family members who had perhaps been sidestepping the issue are enhanced, and trust in the caring doctor is consolidated. This leads to better cooperation during the months ahead of unpleasant treatment programs or palliative care. And, of course, on a practical basis, terminally ill patients can plan ahead for the remaining period of their life, be at ease with their loved ones, and settle financial issues. When the time comes, they can recite the prayers of confession (*vidui*).

As an ophthalmologist, I am rarely the first to diagnose the Big Worry among my patients. I do see patients, of course, with serious illnesses, especially when the eye is involved in the disease process. Patients are usually already aware of their condition and fully counseled when they enter my office, but that doesn't stop the flow of questions.

Occasionally, the diagnosis of an eye complication — such as a cancer metastasis that has spread to the back of the eye — is the first sign that the patient's days may be becoming increasingly numbered. Informing a patient of this new finding is difficult. I know in advance that I may not be equipped to answer the ensuing queries about prognosis and changes in the cancer treatment. I have to be aware of my limitations and not say too much. Some doctors choose to say nothing and merely give the patient a letter for the referring cancer doctor. This, of course, is very risky. In Israel, at least, the patient is bound to open and read the letter with the potential for misunderstandings and unpredictable reactions.

I tend to be as honest as possible, state when I don't know the answer, and try to enhance the patient's confidence in his or her treating physician to whom I refer the patient back for continued care.

I do have to tell patients that they are becoming blind, and such a situation, of course, has to be handled with equal sensitivity. Indeed, some patients are influenced by the rabbinic adage that a blind person is considered dead (*Nedarim* 64b), although usually this is interpreted as meaning that a blind person is at risk of death because of the possibility of falling, etc. In fact, most patients who are classified as "legally blind" do retain some vision, and the patient who sees complete darkness in both eyes is relatively rare.

I always look for a way to give some sense of hope, whether by saying that the condition won't get any worse, or can improve over many months, or that new treatments are being tested. I try not to raise false expectations, but it's a fact that many people live fulfilling lives after going blind, and my job is to encourage patients to enter that group by giving the appropriate medical or surgical treatment if it exists, or referring for visual aids, social workers, counselors, and support groups.

Only recently, a colleague reported at a conference of an incident in which a patient was diagnosed with glaucoma. Five minutes after receiving the diagnosis, the patient was found in the restrooms taking an overdose, convinced mistakenly that she would be completely blind within months. Her father had in fact gone blind due to glaucoma many years before, and due to inadequate counseling by the informing doctor, the patient assumed this would automatically happen to her. She was rapidly reassured that glaucoma, although a potentially blinding disease, is usually treatable when caught early, as in her case. Hope was restored.

When breaking bad news it also helps to know the background of the patient, and if possible, have someone to accompany the patient. Communication is often problematic in stressful situations. Patients regularly miss half of what is said, misunderstand other aspects and even imagine facts that were never stated. A relative or friend can often go through issues again afterward.

Israel is very advanced medically, with Western standards of diagnosis and treatment. Most patients receive their medical care through the public health service, based on four not-for-profit insurance companies. Access to specialists is very direct and inexpensive, and as a result, many patients will seek second and third opinions before accepting that they have a Big Worry and before deciding what to do about it. In addition, patients can often bypass family doctors, unlike the UK medical system for example, where access to specialists is controlled by family doctors.

Israel is a relatively small country, which leads to a situation where news travels fast within communities. People will journey the length of the country (usually no more than two to three hours) to see a specific doctor who once treated some neighbor's distant cousin. All this can lead to a situation of information overload.

Another source of help in Israel during personal health crises is a number of Jewish religiously-based initiatives run by volunteers. One notable organization is run by Rabbi Avraham Elimelech Firer, a Belzer Chassid, and it's called "Ezra Lemarpeh," which he founded in 1979.

History relates that Rabbi Firer was initially moved by the distress of a fellow yeshivah student who was unable to acquire a specific piece of medical equipment. He took it upon himself to raise funds and acquire the instrument from abroad, and after this success, others started asking him for help. From such a mundane beginning, a whole patient-help organization developed, which now offers numerous services, including: a referral and second opinion service, counseling and emotional support, medical education and instruction department, lending of medical equipment, rehabilitation center, hosting healthy children whose parents are hospitalized, and more. All services are free and available to all citizens whether religious, secular, Jewish or non-Jewish.

In particular, what is so remarkable is that many

patients with Big Worries come to Rabbi Firer for medical advice, and he has become a mainstream address within the Israeli medical scene. Rabbi Firer does not treat patients himself and isn't licensed to practice medicine. However, despite being completely self-taught, he has proven his ability over the years to grasp the essence of the medical problems presented to him. He can assess the patient's file and test results and is then able to recommend the best doctor in Israel with the most experience in a particular field, or occasionally abroad. (There are few medical problems today that are not treated in Israel. The exceptions are extremely rare conditions that, owing to Israel's small population, are encountered very infrequently and as a result, Israeli doctors are unable to gain the required expertise.)

Rabbi Firer describes his role below (from the website http://www.ezra-lemarpe.org/content/view/46/258/lang,us):

"The junction where I find myself, along with the rest of Ezra Lemarpeh volunteers, is different. Our encounter with the patients and their families comes about due to their own initiative, following a prior encounter with the Health Services System. Sometimes, this initiative testifies of a lack in their self-confidence, since otherwise they would not have made the effort, at a time which is already full of worry and problems.

People come to us not in order to find cure for a

disease or to get a prescription; people come to us to find encouragement and advice, to strengthen their feeling of trust and confidence for further management of an illness. They wish to know whether the road that is being offered to them is indeed the right one, or whether they should look elsewhere, by a different doctor, at another center, or using a different method of treatment."

His decisions are widely respected also by the medical profession itself. Senior doctors admire his encyclopedic knowledge not just of their specific field, but of all fields of medicine, freely quoting medical research papers and at home with all the medical jargon. On an average day, he sees some forty patients for advice in his office and speaks to a further eighty to ninety over the phone.

Israel, in many ways, reflects on a national scale smaller Diaspora Jewish communities. Another way this is seen is in the functioning of *gemachim* on a national scale, which abroad mainly function internally within *Chareidi* communities. A *gemach* (plural *gemachim*) is short for *gemilut chassadim,* translated as "acts of kindness." Money *gemachim* fulfill the Biblical imperative of lending money without charging interest, *You shall lend money to my people...do not lay interest on him* (*Shemos* 22:24), and also, *You shall not give him your money for interest, nor may you give him your food for increase* (*Vayikra* 25:37).

While originally referring to interest-free money loans, today *gemachim* exist for all manner of items imaginable — from baby paraphernalia to loudspeakers, wedding dresses and ladders. One in particular, "Yad Sarah," is a household name in Israel for lending medical equipment to those in need. Up to 250,000 items, from walking sticks and wheelchairs, to orthopedic beds and specialized electronic equipment, are lent out each year from branches all over the country, free of charge. Any citizen is eligible, Jew or non-Jew, and although no money exchanges hands, two guarantors are usually required in case expensive items are lost or broken.

A person's reaction to a Big Worry is always colored by his life's experiences, which in turn are influenced by the prevailing culture in which he grew up, and his philosophical beliefs. Big Worries can take different forms, not just a serious terminal disease. Another example might be discovering the birth of a handicapped child.

Today this kind of potentially lifelong Big Worry can often be prevented by antenatal screening, but uptake of such testing is very variable among Israel's various communities. For example, members of Israel's religious communities, especially Jewish and Muslim, tend to take fewer antenatal tests, as they are unlikely to request a termination of pregnancy should an abnormal fetus be discovered. There is little point screening for Down Syndrome if you are not going to act on a positive result. Moreover, performing certain tests such as a paracentesis, to withdraw fluid from around the baby within the womb, may actually carry a risk to the fetus. Children with disabilities or autism, for example, are viewed with much more acceptance by observant families as Divine decrees, with different implications. They are not necessarily perceived as Big Worries in the same way that others see such events.

In contrast, secular families, who find the birth of an abnormal baby a much greater emotional challenge, are far more likely to undergo all antenatal testing, and opt for a termination should a serious problem be found.

The long-term management of a child with learning difficulties also varies between Israel's different communities. An Arab pediatrician colleague who works within both the Jewish and Arab communities explained: Jewish parents, upon discovering their child is handicapped, will seek out the best education and services available. They will devote themselves to maximizing their child's potential. Within the Arab community, there is much more denial. A handicapped child is a stigma on the family, and rather than send the child out to therapists and educators, he is often kept at home and looked after within the extended family. The head nurse — also an Arab — at a local Jewish retirement home, confirmed this. She told me of a teacher at a high school in her village, who used to take her Down Syndrome son outside the village for care, rather than let her neighbors see the child. However, as Israel's Arab community becomes more and more westernized and influenced by the Jewish majority, as in other aspects of life, things will hopefully change in this area too.

Healthcare in Israel is probably the area in which Jews and Arabs are most integrated, with Arabs using Jewish doctors, and Jewish patients using Arab doctors. This can lead to complicated scenarios, for instance, after a terror attack in which the terrorist and his victims have been treated within the hospital Emergency Department, in adjacent beds, by mixed Jewish and Arab medical teams. Coping with Big Worries in such a situation can be doubly difficult.

In Israel, emotions run high in stressful situations and are expressed at full volume. Family members of seriously ill hospital patients often camp out in waiting rooms day and night, wanting to be near their loved one, offering him and each other support. The family comes together. The religious recite Psalms, the secular suddenly don *kippot*. Reactions of family members can be unexpectedly explosive; flailing of arms, screams and fainting, far from the dignified and reserved reactions to bad news seen in other societies. Here, this has to be accepted as part of dealing with a Big Worry.

The need to help those of us with a Big Worry is a universal issue in all societies, and for sure there is a right and a wrong way of going about it, depending on many factors. We can all learn from each other. Economic factors play their part too, and indeed there is always room for improvement, in Israel as anywhere else. However, we have, by international comparison, a very effective national health service, and our spirit of volunteering and national service is very strong. I think this is something we can be proud of.

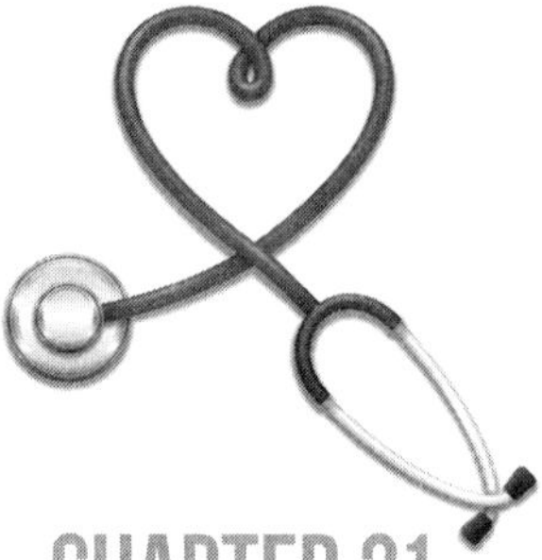

CHAPTER 21

An American Doctor's View

Ruth L. Katz is the Professor of Pathology and Chief Image Analysis Laboratory at MD Anderson Cancer Center, Houston, Texas.

Changing the outlook for cancer, one magic bullet at a time

I have worked at the largest and most famous cancer center in the United States of America for thirty-four years. I have been witness to some remarkable breakthroughs in cancer treatment on so many occasions, that I am now confident that we can change the often dismal prognosis of a cancer sufferer to one of hope for a longer and much better quality life.

As a pathologist and a researcher, I am amazed at the brilliance of our current science in discovering the molecular genetic bases of the causes of cancer, and the innovative drugs that have been developed in the area of targeted therapies." Even a skeptic like myself can start believing in an eventual cure, or a prolonged remission for cancer.

My research interests have been focused predominantly in the field of lung cancer. After receiving a large contract from the National Cancer Institute to study lung cancer some twelve years ago, my husband — then fifty-six years old, was suddenly diagnosed with a fairly advanced lung cancer of the non-small cell type. He had never smoked; however, his father had been a smoker and no doubt he was exposed to second-hand smoke, as well as having a family history with close relatives dying at early ages from different malignancies. The combination of cancer predisposing genes and environmental factors is frequently a potent mix that renders an individual at high risk to develop cancer.

My husband had been coughing softly for a few weeks and when we were in Yosemite National Park, I noticed that I walked ahead of him and he had a hard time keeping up. The cough reminded me of a dear friend, who had recently died of colon cancer that had spread to the lungs, and I referred my husband to my hospital for a chest X-ray. The pulmonologist immediately summoned me to look at the chest films with him, and as I looked at the large mass in his lungs, I realized with a sinking feeling that he would be dead within a couple of years.

The whole course of his treatment — from pre-operative chemotherapy with platinum and Taxol compounds, to a thoracotomy where they could not remove the tumor, to post-operative chemotherapy and radiation — was a horrendous experience for both him and the entire family. He ultimately died eighteen months after diagnosis. I recall to this day the extreme pain and discomfort that he was in following the thoracotomy, where they had to cut through the ribs to open the chest, and ultimately could not remove the tumor because the cancer was too advanced and invaded vital structures.

Unfortunately, his cancer developed just a few months before the onset of the wave of new mutations and their accompanying small-molecule therapies were discovered, which revolutionized the treatment of lung cancer.

I remember questioning his oncologist whether he could not possibly try some of the new anti-epidermal growth factor EGFR inhibitory drugs on my husband, but was told that these were still in an "experimental" stage. After his death in 2001, I was determined to continue to work in the field of lung cancer, which still is the malignancy with the highest incidence, even among non-smokers, and is the one most lethal of all tumors. I wanted to make a contribution to understanding the pathogenesis or the events leading to this disease. There was a need to develop markers for early detection of lung cancer — from a few drops of blood — so that, if caught early enough, a patient could have a small tumor removed and immediately be assured of a better prognosis.

Pathogenesis (the underlying cause) of Cancer

To begin, we need to gain insight into the biological processes that result in a single cancer cell growing and multiplying in an unregulated fashion to form a mass of "crazy" or "malignant" cells, that in turn spawn millions of the same cells to migrate into the bloodstream where they constantly circulate, eventually to implant and grow as the tumor "metastases" in other organs, until eventually the body is overwhelmed and death occurs.

I know that there are millions of these genetically abnormal "crazy" cells in the bloodstream of cancer patients, as I personally made this discovery in my research laboratory about three years ago. Several years previously, I had been working on a library of novel DNA probes which, together with my brilliant colleague, Dr. Feng Jiang, a urologist from China who had recently completed a PhD in molecular biology with a very famous group of researchers from Switzerland. I had hired Feng several years previously, when I first received a large award from N.I.H. to study lung cancer.

In retrospect, it was the most strategic scientific move that I could have made. Feng was well versed in the latest molecular technology methods and we developed novel DNA probes from a small series of lung cancers that had been removed from patients. Through a process known as CGH, or Comparative Genomic Hybridization, we had discovered certain genes that invariably were deleted or lost in lung cancer cells. However, we discovered that these genes were also deleted in the normal cells surrounding the cancer, as well as in the bloodstream of patients with lung cancer.

We performed a novel DNA "FISH" (fluorescence-in-situ hybridization) test on blood samples from subjects with lung cancer, and compared the results with the blood samples from subjects of a similar age group and smoking history (controls), but without cancer. It was my "Eureka! moment" — we showed that there were thousands of cells in the blood that had lost those genes, and possessed the same genetic abnormalities as occurred in the original lung cancer cells. These abnormal cells were the circulating tumor cells, shed from the primary tumor, which were present at significantly higher levels in cancer patients compared to the control subjects. We discovered far more of these cells than had ever been reported, and in fact, in certain patients with advanced disease, we noticed that the number of circulating malignant cells in the blood was very large.

This study was published in *Clinical Cancer Research* in 2010, a prestigious medical journal that is widely circulated. The journal held a national press conference, hosted by experts in the field of lung cancer, who stated that if we could validate our findings in a second, much larger study, this would represent a major breakthrough in the understanding of the biology of lung cancer.

Since that time, we have also been working on breast cancer, and have shown similar findings. I believe that all solid tumors actually manifest thousands of abnormal circulating cells. Based on this and other similar studies, blood is now known as a "liquid biopsy," because we can derive the unique abnormalities, including mutations, of different tumors from a simple blood sample, without resorting to a biopsy. This will keep alive the hope of saving patients with advanced tumors from having to undergo dangerous invasive procedures to obtain tumor tissue.

What Is Cancer, Really?

Cancer is not one big monolithic disease. Every organ system has multiple different types of cancer. The most common ones are, unfortunately, some of the deadliest, especially lung cancer, pancreatic cancer, breast cancer, ovarian, and colo-rectal cancer — the so-called solid tumors. Other types of cancers are the blood-based (hematological malignancies), like the leukemias and lymphomas, of which certain types grow slowly or are "indolent," with the patient living for many years. A leukemia called chronic lymphocytic leukemia is a prime example of a very slow-growing cancer that may be left untreated for many years. Other types of leukemias and lymphomas, however, may be more aggressive and grow rapidly and require multi-agent chemotherapy to control their spread.

Some types of cancers have a better prognosis; for example, "germ"-cell tumors of ovaries and testicles have excellent cures or remission rates if patients can be treated with combination chemotherapy. Testicular tumors such as seminomas are potentially curable by means of high-dose chemotherapy.

Lance Armstrong, the famous cyclist who won many awards, developed a rare and highly dangerous form of testicular cancer called choriocarcinoma at age twenty-five. Initially, Lance discovered a swelling in his testicle, which he tried to ignore. Eventually he saw a urologist who removed the testicle, and subsequently the diagnosis of choriocarcinoma was made. Later, it was discovered that the tumor had metastasized to his lungs and his brain, and he was given only a forty-percent chance of survival. As he wrote in his famous book, *It Is Not About the Bike*, "Of course, I should have known that something was wrong with me. But athletes, especially cyclists, are in the business of denial. Everything hurts. Your back hurts, your feet hurt, your hands hurt, your neck hurts, your legs hurt... So no, I didn't pay attention to the fact that I didn't feel well in 1996. When my right testicle became slightly swollen that winter, I told myself to live with it, because I assumed it was something I had done to myself on the bike, or that my system was compensating for some physiological male thing."

Once Lance discovered that he had testicular cancer, he was proactive about his disease, and after researching the disease, he went to consult with the famous Dr. Lawrence H. Einhorn of the University of Indiana, at the Walther Cancer Institute. There, Lance Armstrong underwent surgery to remove the brain tumors, and then underwent a course of intensive chemotherapy to eradicate the lung metastases.

One year later, Lance was back racing competitively, making one of the most spectacular comebacks in the history of competitive sports. (This is notwithstanding the allegations of his having taken performance-enhancing drugs. Recovering to such an extent and from such a serious diagnosis, which had nothing to do with the drugs that he took, is remarkable by all standards.)

In 1997 Armstrong founded the Lance Armstrong Foundation, which supports people affected by cancer.

The foundation has raised more than $325 million from the sale of yellow Livestrong bracelets. Thus, here we have an amazing example of a strong-willed individual who was able to overcome a dreadfully aggressive cancer by researching assiduously to find the right cancer specialist, and then being fortunate enough to be treated by him.

Heterogeneity of Cancer

Even within one tumor, there are multiple different clones of tumor cells with different numbers of chromosomes and varying mutations. This is known as cancer heterogeneity. Mutation is a very important concept in cancer. It refers to a change in the coding sequence of the genes that results in a deleterious event that may change the normal homeostasis (functional environment) of the cell.

As the tumor grows, cancer stem-cells — which are like the normal stem-cells within our different organs but have now acquired mutations — will develop and multiply, ultimately seeding the bloodstream. These mutations can be due to environmental causes such as tobacco smoke, or chronic inflammation, or mutations that are virally induced by oncogenic (cancer-forming) viruses such as the Human Papilloma Virus. This virus is sexually transmitted and can result in cervical cancer.

Mutations can be due to hereditary factors, such as the

genes brca1/brca2 that can cause breast cancer or ovarian cancer and are carried by a small percentage of Ashkenazi Jews. The cancer stem-cells replicate themselves, with some remaining as primitive cells eternally replicating, as well as giving rise to more differentiated tumor cells resulting in a tumor mass. These cancer stem-cells are actually the progenitors of the malignancy and carry the "driver" genes, otherwise known as "oncogenes," that force the cells to multiply in an unregulated fashion.

A classic example of one of these oncogenes is EGFR, or Epidermal Growth Factor Receptor, which is found in a variety of tumors, including breast, colon, lung, and pancreatic cancer. Within the cancer cell, the gene that transcribes EGFR becomes amplified, or increased in activity, due to multiple copies of the gene being produced. This amplified EGFR is known as the "driver" of the cell. It results in the formation of multiple receptors on the cell membrane, which are structured to interact with the appropriate ligand, or binding protein, from the surrounding environment.

The ligand known as Epidermal Growth Factor (discovered by Stanley Cohen of Vanderbilt University, along with Rita Levi-Montalcini, for which both received the Nobel Prize in Physiology or Medicine in 1986) is captured on the cell surface. Once the ligand interacts with the receptor, the resulting reaction activates multiple different genetic pathways within the cell.

Imagine an electrical current, that when turned on by a flick of a switch, will immediately illuminate a large room by lighting up many light bulbs scattered around the center and circumference of the room. So too, will the Epidermal Growth Factor-ligand interaction instantly activate numerous downstream biochemical reactions within the cell, through specific signaling pathways. Once switched on, activation of pathways occurs, and the cancer cells start to divide continuously and develop ways to prevent cell death. The cancer cells also become "immortalized" through elongation of the ends of chromosomes known as telomeres, which also permits the cells to multiply continuously. (By the way, researchers all over the world would love to exploit the mechanisms involved in this immortalization process, as it is the secret of eternal youth and old age.)

The Miracle of Discovering the Achilles' Heel of Malignancy

The powerful EGFR driver is needed to push cell multiplication forward, and the cells become addicted to this oncogene for their growth. At the same time, if the "driver" is knocked down, the cells will die. For this reason, cancer research is centered on finding the different "drivers" for the many different tumors, and discovering drugs to render the driver impotent.

At a wedding about five years ago, I sat at a table with a

middle-aged couple who were both prominent professors of literature at a university, and were well known in the city. They were also quite religious and active in one of our Orthodox synagogues. When the dancing began, the husband excused himself to go and join the men in dancing a rather hectic "*Horah*" around the *chattan* (groom), and then proceeded to grab the groom's arm and together they twirled around at breakneck speed.

His wife came to sit next to me while he was dancing, and confided in me that several years before, he had been very ill, and had advanced stage IV non-small cell lung cancer, which had spread throughout the body. He had almost exhausted all his chemotherapy options.

A few months prior to the onset of his cancer, scientists had discovered that there were mutations within certain regions of the EGFR receptor that were susceptible to the effects of a tyrosine kinase inhibitor (TKI) called Erlotinib or Gefitinib. This was a small molecule that "interacted" with the site where the enzyme was active, and in so doing was able to silence the downstream effects that resulted in the aggressive nature of the cancer cells. The drug could be given orally, and it was only given to cancer patients who tested positive for this EGFR mutation.

At that time, most of the lung cancer patients who tested positive for the mutation were usually Asian women who had never smoked. Fortunately, her husband tested positive for one of the EGFR mutations, and on receiving the TKI therapy, almost immediately began to experience a rapid relief in his symptoms. He stopped his chronic coughing, began breathing more easily, and began to put on weight. His radiology studies showed dramatic improvement with almost complete remission of the tumor throughout his body.

What had occurred was that the "driver" oncogene — in this case the effects of the EGFR mutation — had been blocked by the TKI, and the malignant cells now had the activating switch thrown into the "off" position. This, in turn, initiated a large cascade of dying cells and reduction in tumor volume. Within a few weeks, the radiology studies showed a total disappearance of the cancer. The man had now regained his life, his strength, and his confidence. He was able to be there for his wife, children, and grandchildren, and gained hope for the future. Three years later he is still in remission.

Another dramatic story of targeted therapy delivered in a novel manner occurred several months ago, and concerned a fifty-two-year-old woman with breast cancer at such an advanced stage that it had spread into her brain and spinal cord. The MRI showed that the spinal cord, especially toward the lower back, was encased with tumor. The usual survival time for patients in this situation is about twelve weeks. The lady was highly intelligent — she loved to run marathons, and practiced yoga daily.

Knowing that this patient had a fairly common oncogene "driver" called Her2neu that was over-expressed in her primary breast cancer and metastatic tumor cells, we demonstrated that the cerebrospinal fluid contained malignant breast cancer cells with the same amplified Her2neu gene. In this case, the Her2neu gene was the "driver" and we knew that if we knocked this down we could effect a dramatic response. In my lab, we also reacted these malignant cells with the drug called Herceptin, which precisely targets the cell membrane which bears the Her2neu receptor, and showed that the cells in the spinal fluid were targeted by this drug.

However, we knew that if we delivered this drug in the bloodstream, it would not penetrate through the brain barrier. The only and most logical method to deliver the drug was going to be through a reservoir that had to be inserted in her brain to connect to the spinal fluid. At the same time, we showed that she had thousands of malignant cells in her bloodstream that also expressed the oncogene Her2neu.

After getting special permission from the president of our hospital to treat this patient "off protocol," and to administer this drug directly into the brain, we began to treat the woman twice weekly with a combination of intrathecal (into the spinal cord) and intravenous Herceptin, in combination with another chemotherapy agent.

After three weeks of treatment, Dr. Loghin, her neuro-oncologist, sent me the repeat PET/CT scan and the MRI... My eyes filled with tears as I saw that the tumor had completely disappeared in the spinal cord and the brain. We also showed that all the malignant circulating cells had been cleared from the blood.

This woman, thirty weeks from the first treatment, is feeling well, running daily, and continuing with her daily yoga. She had an amazing will to live, and extreme courage to subject herself to therapy that was "experimental." She is a true trailblazer, and based on her remarkable result, our breast oncologist has submitted a grant proposal to a large pharmaceutical company. We have requested funding for a larger study in which more patients with breast cancer metastatic to the brain — which is uniformly associated with a rapid onset of death — will receive a similar treatment.

I have been very fortunate to be at an institute where we have some brilliant oncologists who can think "out of the box" and come up with a new approach to treat and target cancer, including types where until recently, there has been very little progress.

One such person is Dr. Razelle Kurzrock, who, several years ago, started testing many different kinds of cancers for different mutations, and then treating the mutations with new drugs especially designed for these mutations. She has obtained remarkable results with cancers that are advanced and refractory to conventional chemotherapies. Her large series of patients that she has treated in this way have much higher remission rates and much lower progression rates than patients treated by standard non-targeted chemotherapy.

Current standard care practices are to test for the common oncogenes that have "actionable" targets, meaning that once we identify in a particular tumor that such a defect or oncogene is active, we can now give the appropriate drug for that tumor, known also as "personalized" medicine. Examples of these are mutations in EGFR, KRAS, BRAF, ALK-EML (fusion), Ret oncogene, PIK3CA, and many others. What lies in the future is next-generation sequencing of the cancer patient's DNA. Every cancer patient will have their cancers sequenced... and thousands of genes will be examined for mutations or translocations of genes, and the appropriate therapies to target these abnormalities will be given.

New technologies that previously took months to examine the human genome, are now taking weeks and soon days to complete. As the technology improves, the cost of the testing becomes much more reasonable and well within the reach of most patients, regardless of financial or socioeconomic status.

For the first time in the history of cancer, we are seeing a bright light on the horizon. All cancer patients need to know that there are programs such as Dr. Kurzrock's program at MD Anderson Cancer Center that exist, and that are open to all who are interested. So hopefully Big Worries can now become smaller worries as we enter into a new enlightened age where, with Hashem's help, we can continue to shine a light on treating cancer patients, enabling good quality of life and longer life.

CHAPTER 22

Resources and Help

I think one of the most difficult tasks a person could undertake is to compile a list of organizations and individuals in the Jewish community that have been set up to help others with a Big Worry. It is simply too large a list.

Here are a few names and addresses where you might begin to turn for help. There will be many, many others, apart from all the *rabbanim* and their wives, the shuls, doctors, nurses, and other individuals I have not cited or don't even know about.

This list should, though, allow you to at least make a start in finding the people who can help you find the best possible support for a member of your family, a friend or simply someone who asks you for help.

I should point out that Chai Lifeline has evolved far beyond dealing only with cancer-related issues. It now offers a very wide scope of services and support for those suffering with any chronic medical issue, and assists families in coping with trauma and tragedy.

My sincere thanks to Mrs. Zahava Farbman of Chai Lifeline NY, who helped so much in compiling this introduction to the vast resources that represents a part of the *chessed* of Klal Yisrael.

Resources and Help

ISRAEL

Agudat Iyal	02-500-0283	Pediatric Epilepsy
Akim Yerushalayim	02-672-8731	Disabilities
Assif	02-5385691	Premature Babies
Azulei	02-582-7517	Maternity/Nursing
Beis Natan	02-6446052	Women's Health/Cancer
Bikur Cholim – Belz	02-538-1840	General
Bikur Cholim – Neshei Yerushalayim	02-9923707	General
Bonei Olam	052-765-4097	Infertility
Cancer Sufferers Group	02-625-6721	Cancer
Chai Lifeline Jerusalem	02-658-3000	Cancer +
Chessed U'Marpeh	08-9495080	Geriatrics

Darchei Miriam	02-532-5639	Cancer
Ezer Metzion	03-574-2742	General
Ezra LeMarpeh Rav Firer	03-577-7000	General
Gefen Poriah	1-800-210-410	Infertility
Kav L'Chaim	1-700-707-012	Pediatric Cancer
Kesher	1-700-501-601	Special Needs
L'ha V'a	054-844-1833	Kidney
Lev Rachel	02-643-3447	Cancer
Machon Puah	02-651-5050	Infertility
Magen L'Choleh Benny Fisher	02-644-2000	General
Misgav L'Kashish	02-625-2444	Geriatrics
Neta Shorek	077-700-4005	Infertility
Ohr Amram	02-6439039	General/Maternity
Pri Chaim R' Shlesinger	02-500-1501	Infertility
Rachse Leib	08-852-3805	General
Rav Sheinberger	02-538-6142	Family Issues
Rav Tov	02-538-2856	General
Refuah L'Chaim Vizhnitz	03-674-1122	General
Refuah Krovor	02-538-8174	General
Refuah V'Yeshuah Gur	08-8662745	General
Refui V'rapo Yerapeh	072-249-0934	Muscle Problems
Shaare Marpeh	02-581-3558	General
Shiloah	02-651-9555	Special Needs

Telem	02-534-6445	Child Development
Tikve U'Marpe	02-500-2831	Pediatric Dialysis
Yad Ha'Rama	02-571-5727	General
Yismach Leib	1-700-708-017	Physical Handicaps
Zichron Menachem	02-634-3001	Pediatric Cancer
Zir Chemed – Dr. Baruch Brooks	02-653-5395	Infertility

U.S.

Chai Lifeline – East Coast	212-465-1300	Cancer +
Chai Lifeline – West Coast	310-274-6331	Cancer +
Chai Lifeline – Midwest	847-763-1818	Cancer +
Chai Lifeline – New Jersey	732-719-1700	Cancer +
Camp Simcha	212-699-6672 845-856-1432	Cancer +
ECHO Medical Referral Service	718-859-9800 845-425-9570	Medical & Physician Referrals
A TIME	718-437-7110	Infertility
Bonei Olam	718-252-1212 732-942-7773	Infertility
Rofeh Cholim Cancer Society (RCCS)	718-854-5558	Financial/Insurance Assistance
Zichron Shlomo Refuah Fund	718-633-6688	Practical & Emotional Support
Kids of Courage	888-9-KIDSOC	Practical & Emotional Support

Jewish Child Life Society	866-4HELP-CF	Cystic Fibrosis
Jewish Caring Network (JCN) – Baltimore	410-602-6075	Support Services
Rofeh International – Brookline	617-566-1900	Medical Support, Referrals
Chicago Center for Torah and Support	773-761-4005	Medical Referral & Support
L.A. Bikur Cholim – Rabbi Hershey Ten	323-852-1900	
Los Angeles Ladies Bikur Cholim	323-934-2890 323-936-1685	
Puah (L.A. Division) – Mrs. Ahuva Goldstein	323-938-8660 cell: 213-840-7571	Infertility
Refuah Resources – Rabbi Shuki Berman	718-437-7474	

CANADA

Chai Lifeline	647-430-5933	Cancer +

UK

Chai Lifeline	0208-202-9297	Cancer +
Chana	0208-201-8774	Infertility
Kivisi	0161-773-7830	Infertility
Jewish Care Scotland	0141-620-1800	General Support
Norwood	0208-809-8809	General Support

BELGIUM

Chai Lifeline	32-495-198-100	Cancer +

Glossary

A"h: An acronym for "alav hashalom - peace be upon him."

Ashkenazi: Jews originally from Northern and Eastern parts of Europe and Russia

Avos: Forefathers

Baalei tzedakah: One who gives charity

Beis din: Jewish Rabbinical Court of Law

Brachah: Blessing

Chareidi: Ultra-Orthodox

Chassan: Bridegroom

Chazal: Acronym for "chachameinu zichronim livrachah, our Sages of blessed memory"

Cheder: lit.– Room; Religious School for young boys

Chessed: Act of loving kindness

Chevra kaddisha: Jewish burial society

Daas Torah: Rabbinic guidance; Torah viewpoint and perspective

Daven: Pray

Dvar Torah: Words of Torah; Torah thoughts

Frum: "(Yid.) Religious, Torah observent"

G'zar din: Heavenly Decree

Gadol/gedolim: The Spiritual Leader/s of a Generation

Gehinnom: Hell; term used to indicate the place where the soul goes after death for purification

Gemachim: Free lending organizations

Gemara: Talmud

Get: Certificate of Jewish divorce

Haskamah: Approbation

Horah: An Israeli type of dance

Kabbalah: Esoteric teachings of the Torah

Kallah: Bride

Kippot: Skullcaps

Kollel: A place of Torah study generally for married men

Litvish: "lit. "of Lithuanian origin," non-Chassidic sector of religious Jews"

Mashiach: Jewish Messiah

Mazel: Fortune; luck

Meshugah: (Yid.) Crazy

Mitzvos: Torah Commandment/s

Mizrachi: Religious Zionist

Mosad: A charitable foundation

Mussar: Rebuke or the study of Torah ethics and personal discipline

Neshamah: Soul

Niftar: Deceased Person; corpse

Pasuk: Verse from the Torah

Pirkei Tehillim: Chapters of Psalms

Psak: Halachic ruling

Rav/rabbanim: Rabbi/s

Rebbe: Chassidic leader serving also as mentor to a following of chassidim

Rebbetzin: Rabbi's wife

Refuah sheleimah: Complete recovery

Rosh yeshivah: Head or dean of a yeshiva or Torah Institution

Ruach hakodesh: "Divine Inspiration, a lesser form of prophecy"

Sedra: Weekly Torah portion

Sefarim: "Holy, Jewish text(s)"

Seudah shlishis: Third meal of Shabbos, eaten on Shabbos afternoon

Shabbaton: An event or program held over Shabbos

Shalom Aleichem: Peace Unto You (traditional greeting); song welcoming angels Friday evening prior to the Sabbath meal

Shamayim: Heaven/s

Shavuos: Festival of the Harvest in late spring

Sheitel: Wig

Shiurim: Torah Lecture/s

Shivah: Seven-day mourning period

Shlit"a: An acronym for "Sheyichyeh L'yamim Tovim Aruchim, – will live many long and good days"

Shmoozing: Informal conversation

Shul: Synagogue

Simchah: Happiness; Joyous Occasion/s of

Sofer: Scribe

Talmidim: Student/s

Tefillin: Phylacteries

Tikkun: A procedure that has been proscribed by someone of Rabbinical stature, or an occurence that has been pre-ordained by Hashem whose purpose is an atonement

Tzaddik: Righteous individual

Tzara'as: Spiritual disease that is a punishment for lashon hara and other sins

Yeshivah: Place of Torah learning

Zechus: Merit

Zohar: Book of Kabbalah

Zt"l: An acronym for "zecher tzaddik livrachah — may a tzaddik be remembered for blessing."

About the Author

Rabbi Y.Y. Rubinstein learned in Gateshead Yeshivah for seven years, where he received his *semichah,* and then for three years in the Liverpool *kollel.* He has been a regular contributor to *Hamodia* and the UK's *Jewish Tribune,* and has written for several other publications, as well. He lectures all over the world and is a regular broadcaster for BBC Radio and TV. On BBC World Service, he has

been heard by audiences of over 156 million people. Her Majesty Queen Elizabeth has declared herself a fan of Rabbi Rubinstein's broadcasts, saying, "He's awfully good." In a piece called "Mentors," the UK's national *Independent* newspaper cited him as being one of the five people in the UK, along with Tony Blair's mentor, to turn to for advice.

In August of 2011, Rabbi Rubinstein moved to New York. *The Little Book for BIG Worries* is Rabbi Rubinstein's sixth book.